NORTHERN WHITE-CEDAR

NORTHERN WHITE-CEDAR

The Tree of Life

GERALD L. STORM

LAURA S. KENEFIC

MICHIGAN STATE UNIVERSITY PRESS | *East Lansing*

♾ The paper used in this publication meets the minimum requirements of ANSI/NISO
Z39.48-1992 (R 1997) (Permanence of Paper).

Michigan State University Press
East Lansing, Michigan 48823-5245

Library of Congress Cataloging-in-Publication Data
Names: Storm, Gerald L., author. | Kenefic, Laura S. (Laura Susan), 1970- author.
Title: Northern white-cedar : the tree of life / Gerald L. Storm and Laura S. Kenefic.
Description: East Lansing, Michigan : Michigan State University, [2021] |
Includes bibliographical references and index.
Identifiers: LCCN 2021054406 | ISBN 9781611864281 (paperback) | ISBN 9781609176976 (PDF) |
ISBN 9781628954654 (ePub) | ISBN 9781628964592 (Kindle)
Subjects: LCSH: Thuja occidentalis. | Thuja occidentalis--Ecology. | Thuja occidentalis--Conservation.
Classification: LCC SD397.T53 S76 2021 | DDC 634.9/756--dc23/eng/20211110
LC record available at https://lccn.loc.gov/2021054406

Book design by Preston Thomas
Cover design by Preston Thomas
Cover photo: Cedar Trees at Gooseberry Falls, Minnesota,
photograph by Susanne von Schroeder www.soulcenteredphotography.net, used with permission.

Michigan State University Press is a member of the Green Press Initiative and is committed to developing
and encouraging ecologically responsible publishing practices. For more information about the Green Press
Initiative and the use of recycled paper in book publishing, please visit www.greenpressinitiative.org.

Visit Michigan State University Press at www.msupress.org

For my grandsons, Ryan and Addison
—GERALD L. STORM

For my sons, Liam and Evan, and all foresters who hug trees
—LAURA S. KENEFIC

CONTENTS

ACKNOWLEDGMENTS

We gratefully acknowledge the many scientists and natural resource managers whose work on northern white-cedar served as the foundation for this book. In particular, we thank Jeanette Allogio, University of Maine; Emmanuelle Boulfroy, Centre d'enseignement et de recherche en foresterie de Sainte-Foy inc.; Rod Chimner, Michigan Technological University; Christel Kern, U.S. Forest Service; Catherine Larouche, Ministère des Forêts, de la Faune et des Parcs, Quebec; Guy Lessard, Centre d'enseignement et de recherche en foresterie de Sainte-Foy inc.; Charles Tardif, Maibec; Jay Wason, University of Maine; Justin Waskiewicz, Paul Smith's College; and Christopher Woodall, U.S. Forest Service, for contributing sidebars and appendices. We are grateful to Keith R. McCaffery, Wisconsin Department of Natural Resources (retired) for his coauthorship of chapter 6. Reviews and suggestions about earlier versions of the manuscript were provided by Varun Anand, University of Maine; Robin Clark, Michigan Technological University; Patricia and Howard Cody; Andrew Cutko, Maine Bureau of Parks and Lands; Shawn Fraver, University of Maine; Philip Hofmeyer, Morrisville State College; Richard Judd, University of Maine (emeritus); Richard LaValley, Wisconsin Department of Natural Resources (retired); Ryan O'Connor, Wisconsin Department of Natural Resources; KaDonna Randolph, U.S. Forest Service; Jean-Claude Ruel, Laval University; the late Herbert Schotz, Ice Age Trail Alliance; John and Susan Wolslegel; and others. We thank the Menominee Indian Tribe of Wisconsin for allowing us to take photographs of northern white-cedar on their tribal lands and appreciate the help of Nick Hunter; Diane and Ross Morgan; Carla and Tom Storm; and Friedrich Wendorff. We are thankful for support from

Maibec and the U.S. Forest Service, Northern Research Station. Finally, we are indebted to Mike Guerin for his assistance in the final stages of the manuscript writing and editing process, and to Michigan State University Press editors Catherine Cocks and Julie Loehr (retired) for their guidance.

This work was supported in part by the U.S. Forest Service, Northern Research Station. The findings and conclusions in this publication are those of the author(s) and should not be construed to represent any official USDA or U.S. government determination or policy.

PREFACE

LAURA S. KENEFIC

I had been studying northern white-cedar for more than a decade when I got a call in 2013 from Gerald "Jerry" L. Storm in Onalaska, Wisconsin. I had never met Jerry before, and I had no idea where Onalaska was. He said he was a retired wildlife biologist and had watched one of my presentations online. He told me he was writing a book about northern white-cedar and asked if I would like to write it with him. I agreed. Looking back on it now, that was a strange thing for me to do given that I knew nothing about him at the time. But something about talking to Jerry told me that this would be a good idea.

We worked on the book on and off for more than six years. As a retiree, he had more time to invest in the project than I did. At times he may have been frustrated with my lack of progress, but he never showed that frustration and always expressed appreciation for my work. At other times, he could barely keep up when I crammed a month of work into a few days when my schedule cleared. He was always gracious about all my contributions and edits; he told me many times I should be the first author. I demurred. This was Jerry's book, without a doubt.

During the time we worked together he reminisced about the walks he and his wife used to take in the woods. He sent me news and photos of his grandchildren, and updates about where they were and what they were doing. And still we kept working, emailing, and talking on the phone. Jerry sent my boys T-shirts from Pennsylvania, where he used to live, and me stoneware from Minnesota. He sent me letters in the mail with copies of articles or images he wanted to include in the book. I sent him Christmas cards and a sculpture I bought for him in Quebec made from a piece of a northern white-cedar tree collected in the Gaspé Peninsula.

The authors in Wisconsin in 2016. *(Photo by C. Kern)*

Jerry was passionate, well-read, and thoughtful. He couldn't get around in the woods very well anymore and didn't have the opportunity to see many northern white-cedar trees. I told him about all the northern white-cedar we have in Maine and sent him photos from my work. We met only once, when I traveled to Wisconsin for fieldwork and made a side trip to see him. I was able to find him when I arrived at the restaurant because he had a cup with a northern white-cedar branch in it. I brought him a small northern white-cedar seedling from my yard at home. Early in 2020, we were working on yet another revision. Jerry edited a chapter on a Sunday afternoon and emailed it to me. Later that day he had a stroke; he died a few days later with his family around him.

It's hard to explain how much I lost when I lost Jerry. This was our project. It was never my project. It was hard to continue without him, but his family stepped in to help so I didn't have to do it alone. His son Tom sent me his notes and books, and his nephew Mike took over editing and version control. A year later we had a new final draft. Jerry is still the first author as he deserves to be. Jerry wasn't here to finish the book, but he did write about his worries for the future of northern white-cedar:

When it comes to conservation of northern white-cedar, perhaps the foremost need is to make sure that greater numbers of people have the opportunity to learn about the consequences of losing these unique conifer trees and communities. When we lose a plant community with northern white-cedar we lose more than just trees and their aesthetic, ecologic, economic, and recreational values. We lose a slice of the earth's landscape and its natural resources that historically nourished and supported Native Americans and immigrant settlers; a landscape that continues to enrich the lives of current and future generations. We lose a unique, wind-blown northern white-cedar theater featuring a classic predator-prey drama involving the anti-predator behavior of a snowshoe hare and a cunning predator, the bobcat. We lose a chance to witness dynamic ecological processes involving northern white-cedar, balsam fir, and black spruce competing for space in an ever-changing environment. When we lose a population of ancient northern white-cedar in forests or cliffs of the Great Lakes, New England, Appalachia, Ontario, Quebec, or Atlantic Provinces, we lose a species with the genetic make-up to adapt and survive for over 1,000 years in harsh environments.

I hope you, like me, are inspired by Jerry, this book we wrote together, and his love for trees and communities he rarely got to see.

CHAPTER 1

Hidden Depths:
Our Evolving Relationship
with Northern White-Cedar

The most interesting things in life are those that continue to surprise us, like fronds of frost on windowpanes or old desks with secret cubbies. Northern white-cedar is one of those things. If trees had personalities, northern white-cedar would be an introvert. It is unassuming, tending to be small in stature with a narrow crown that respects its neighbors' spaces. It is patient, growing slowly beneath the main canopy of larger trees, and compliant, leaning to the side when weighed down by snow and ice. It is gentle, with leaves arranged in soft sprays rather than sharply pointed needles, and fragile, with weak wood prone to decay when living. But just as people have hidden depths, so too does northern white-cedar. In fact, it isn't even a cedar (see Sidebar 1). Taking a long-term perspective, we find that northern white-cedar is persistent, increasing its growth to take advantage of canopy openings when they occur, sometimes over and over until it emerges into the full sun. It is tenacious, outlasting trees of other species by living for centuries or even a millennium. It is resilient, thriving even with a high proportion of rotten wood, and resourceful,

Old (*left*) and young (*above*) northern white-cedar trees.

finding places to live and grow where other trees don't prosper. Finally, it is constantly reinventing itself with branches that grow roots when resting on the moist ground, transforming into new trees.

Yet just like human relationships, northern white-cedar's relationship with us—and with the plants and animals that make up its natural communities—can be summed up in two words: it's complicated (see Appendices A and B for the common and scientific names of plants and animals mentioned in this book). Prone to decay when living, northern white-cedar is highly resistant to decay when dead. Indigenous peoples have long used its lightweight, rot-resistant wood and branches for a multitude of everyday items, including woven bags, floor coverings, arrow shafts, and canoe ribs. They extract medicine from the leaves and bark to treat a variety of illnesses and shared this knowledge with early explorers and European settlers in North America. In fact, the chemical constituents of northern white-cedar have pharmacological properties and are rich in vitamin C. A Haudenosaunee decoction of northern white-cedar is credited with saving the French explorer Jacques Cartier's crew from scurvy when their ship was locked in ice near Quebec, Canada, in the winter of 1535. He was so impressed with the tree's curative powers that he brought its seeds to France as a gift for King Francis I (Moore 1978).

SIDEBAR 1   A Case of Mistaken Identity

Northern white-cedar, western redcedar, and Cedar of Lebanon. *(Illustration by Michael A. Klafke)*

You might be surprised to learn that this book isn't about a cedar tree. The actual cedars—of which there are four species—all live in the Mediterranean basin and Himalayas and are in the pine (*Pinaceae*) family. The best-known of these is Cedar of Lebanon, which featured prominently in the Bible. That species was prized by ancient Phoenicians and used in ceremonies, shipbuilding, and construction. Cedar of Lebanon is a fragrant evergreen tree with durable and decay-resistant wood. That tree and its three brethren are the only true cedars. The reason northern white-cedar is called a cedar when it isn't a cedar can be traced back to ancient Greece. It all began with a misunderstanding that is now regarded as "a major embarrassment" (Meiggs 1982) and that caused confusion about species' names that has persisted until today. Here is how it happened:

The name *cedar* is from the word *kedros*, which is what the ancient Greeks called junipers. Junipers are also fragrant evergreen trees with durable and decay-resistant wood. It is believed that when the Greeks first encountered the wood of the true cedars, they called it kedros because it was similar to the juniper wood they knew well (Meiggs 1982). Based on the Greeks' influence, kedros (*cedrus* in Latin, and later *cedar* in English) became a commonly used name for both junipers and cedars around the world. This included the true cedars as well as other species in the Cypress (*Cupressaceae*) family. One such tree is northern white-cedar, also a fragrant evergreen tree with durable and decay-resistant wood. The hyphen between the words white and cedar is used to indicate that it is not a true cedar.

Northern white-cedar and similar trees in the Cypress family (including its giant cousin, western redcedar) have been described as "so-called cedars" or "false cedars." Though they may not be cedars in term of their taxonomy (scientific classification), we should not let their exclusion from the club of true cedars diminish our appreciation for their unique characteristics and importance to the many communities—plant, wildlife, and human—in which they live.

Northern white-cedar was planted in the royal gardens at Fontainebleau and became known as *l'arbre de vie* (*arbor vitae* or *arborvitae* in Latin): the tree of life.

Yet while northern white-cedar was esteemed by sixteenth-century French royalty and is sacred to many Indigenous peoples, this reverence did not transfer with its utility to European settlers in North America. Greatly valuing the tree for shakes and shingles, log homes, fence posts, and furniture, European settlers harvested so much northern white-cedar that they reduced its abundance throughout its range. This isn't just a problem for the species itself. In addition to meeting the needs of people, northern white-cedar provides habitat for many different species of wildlife and plants. Rare orchids such as the showy lady's slipper—described by Brandenburg (2003) as "more spectacular than a fireworks display"—make their homes beneath its canopy. Flying squirrels have been known to travel long distances to strip the insect-repelling bark for their nests (Patterson et al. 2007). White-tailed deer, in particular, rely on dense stands of northern white-cedar for protection from winter snow and wind. Yet those very same deer—driven in some places to overpopulation by extirpation of predators such as mountain lions and gray wolves, human land use, and wildlife management policies—eat so many small northern white-cedar that many stands are unable to regenerate. Too often, seedlings start to grow but are so heavily browsed they never become full-size trees.

Showy lady's slipper. *(Photo by Chelsea Kieffer)*

Today, northern white-cedar is an aging resource without enough successful offspring to sustain the species in all the places it has grown in the past (see Appendix C). And because northern white-cedar trees tend to grow very slowly—often taking a century to grow large enough to be used as a fence post—most of the small trees of today won't reach the canopy for many years (Larouche et al. 2010). Adding insult to injury, road construction and real estate development disrupt water flow in forested wetlands where northern white-cedar is common, causing some stands to die from too much water and others from too little. Nonnative plants like glossy buckthorn can invade the understories of northern white-cedar stands (Smith 2017), usurping space needed for new tree seedlings. Even where northern white-cedar is growing well, scientists predict that future climate will be inhospitable to its regeneration and growth in many places where it grows now, relegating it to the category of climate change "loser" (Iverson et al. 2008).

But there is more to this story than bad news. Northern white-cedar remains common—even abundant—in parts of the northeastern and north-central United States and across the border in Quebec and Ontario, Canada. It grows in nearly pure, dense stands in swamps and seeps, scattered among other trees on gentle slopes with rich mineral soil, and clinging to rock faces on cliffs and bluffs. Stands of northern white-cedar are even found on abandoned pasturelands, where its seedlings were more successful than those of other species at withstanding trampling by cattle (de Blois and Bouchard 1995). And because

Northern white-cedar stands in Témiscamingue (*left*), Quebec, and an old field in Vermont (*above*). (*Quebec photo by Catherine Larouche*)

northern white-cedar plays an integral part in our lives, many people have great affection for it. Northern white-cedar is associated with things we hold dear to our hearts, like hope chests and rustic cabins. The scent of its essential oils is processed in the same parts of our brains as emotions and memories. It is perhaps not surprising that even people who know little of trees and forests care about northern white-cedar.

Nevertheless, having and enjoying northern white-cedar trees today doesn't mean we will have them to enjoy in the future. We need only look to Nova Scotia, Canada, for a cautionary tale. Northern white-cedar is rare in that province today, with a limited and highly fragmented population. It is listed as vulnerable under the Nova Scotia Endangered Species Act of 1998 (Nova Scotia DNR 2010). Yet historical records and archeological evidence suggest this species was more common before European settlers arrived (Johnson 1986). Early explorers described stands of northern white-cedar trees in Nova Scotia, and Mi'kmaq people used the wood for arrows and canoes. A sixteenth-century basket made from northern white-cedar was discovered in a Mi'kmaq grave near the present-day town of Pictou, Nova Scotia (Gordon 1993). Basketweavers of that First Nation today still use the same weaving techniques, but no longer use northern white-cedar.

Today, northern white-cedar forests on provincial land in Nova Scotia are reserved from harvesting because of their rarity. In the Lake States of the United States, northern white-cedar forests are not rare, but regeneration and recruitment failures (when seedlings fail to establish or grow to larger sizes) are common. In fact, many foresters in areas of high deer populations have been discouraged by the lack of successful northern white-cedar regeneration and recruitment after harvesting. Similar problems have occurred in parts of Maine and New Brunswick. Without young northern white-cedar trees to make up the new stand, shrubs or trees of other species predominate, changing the character of the forest. This has led some public agencies to impose moratoria on northern white-cedar harvesting on the lands they manage. Even on privately owned lands, some northern white-cedar stands are designated as deer wintering areas (deer yards) and subject to regulation by state wildlife agencies. This may result in less harvesting if regeneration success is uncertain. While not harvesting trees does maintain the mature trees already on the landscape, it does not resolve the problem of how to ensure that there will be northern white-cedar in the future. Though some thousand-year-old northern white-cedar trees have been found on cliffs on the Niagara Escarpment in Ontario, Canada (Larson and Kelly

1991), most northern white-cedar on the landscape today live for less than a few hundred years. Northern white-cedar is a lot of things, but it is not immortal.

For all these reasons, now is the time to consider the future of northern white-cedar, the natural communities it supports, and the many services it provides to people. We know that this species has unique cultural, ecological, and economic values, but we have nevertheless long extracted usable northern white-cedar trees from the forest without paying enough attention to the quality and quantity of those left behind. Though common in the forests of northeastern and north-central United States and Canada, northern white-cedar remains one of the least-studied commercial tree species in North America (Hofmeyer et al. 2007). There are still a lot of things we don't know about northern white-cedar and the complex relationships it has with other living things, though we rely on the many services it provides. A telling example is the story of Manidoo-giizhikens (Spirit Little Cedar Tree), a lone gnarled northern white-cedar growing for at least four hundred years on Ojibwe lands on the rocky shoreline of Lake Superior. The site of this tree, though sacred to Ojibwe people, was open to the public until vandalism threatened the tree's survival (WCCO 2015). Grand Portage Band members now act as guides to prevent people from removing pieces of the tree for their own use. The metaphor is obvious: without the thoughtful stewardship of humans, we run the risk of asking too much not only of the Spirit Little Cedar Tree, but of northern white-cedar more generally.

To help remedy these problems, we have taken a close look at what we know about northern white-cedar and its natural communities, and what we still need to learn about its ecological complexity and management. In the following pages, you will be introduced—or reintroduced—to northern white-cedar (see Sidebar 2). Whether this tree is a new acquaintance or an old friend, there is much to learn about the places it lives, the company it keeps, and the challenges and opportunities it faces over the course of its life from seed to old-growth tree. We will take a long view, from post-glacial range expansion to projected climate change impacts. This journey will take us from the Atlantic coast to the shores of the Great Lakes, exploring the places—from low swamps to high cliffs—where northern white-cedar has put down roots. We will stop along the way to consider the many values and uses of northern white-cedar, not just for humankind but for the many plants and animals that make up its communities. We will explore avenues for

Spirit Little Cedar Tree. *(Photo by Susanne von Schroeder)*

sustainable management, guided by lessons learned from scientists and natural resource managers.

While we make this trip together, we hope that you will reflect on the ways northern white-cedar has touched your life. Do you have a cedar hope chest, moth-repellent cedar in your closet, cedar siding on your home, cedar patio furniture, or cedar mulch in your gardens? Have you hiked in forests where northern white-cedar trees grow, or hunted wildlife—with a camera or a gun—that shelter in northern white-cedar trees or stands? Or is it enough to know that these things and these places exist, contributing importantly to the richness of life where they are found? If so, what can you do to ensure that northern white-cedar is used sustainably and that these trees and forests will thrive long into the future?

We hope this book will ignite a fresh public attitude toward sound stewardship of northern white-cedar, and more generally toward native natural resources: an attitude that considers multiple species and recognizes the many levels of natural resource management, from individual trees to landscapes. Our goal is to arouse public interest in the values of northern white-cedar communities, and to draw attention to the need to recognize and mitigate threats to sustainability of this species. We aren't the first ones to make this appeal. In 1990, Michigan

State University professor Raymond Miller gave a presentation at a workshop in Ontario, Canada, about managing northern white-cedar. He lamented that "We have a cedar resource that is aging, deer herds are larger now than ever before, and stumpage prices for cedar increase every year. The pressure on this resource has never been higher and if things continue as they are, it is certainly doomed." He concluded his presentation by asking: "Is the cedar resource (and its associated wildlife, watershed, and timber values) important enough that we make room on our list of priorities to save it?" It is our hope that this book will motivate you to join in answering, "Yes."

SIDEBAR 2   How to Recognize Northern White-Cedar

JUSTIN WASKIEWICZ

Northern white-cedar is one of five Cypress family species native to the eastern United States and Canada. These five are radically different from all other native trees in the area, so can be mistaken only for each other. Two are shrubs (common and creeping juniper) and the other three (northern white-cedar, Atlantic white-cedar, and eastern redcedar) have limited range overlap. Thus, in most of the area where it grows, northern white-cedar is easy to recognize.

Leaves

Northern white-cedar has tiny leaves, called *scale* leaves because they are tightly pressed to the twig, overlapping each other and covering the twig surfaces completely the way scales cover a reptile's skin. The individual leaves are only about an eighth-inch (0.3 cm) long and half as wide, and are quite difficult to separate and examine individually. Flat sprays of branching twigs bear hundreds of scale leaves, and these flat sprays, by the hundreds themselves, form the tree crown. The only other trees native to northern white-cedar's range that also bear scale leaves are other members of the Cypress family.

Northern white-cedar leaves.

Northern white-cedar bark (*left*). Northern white-cedar cones (*right*). *(Photo by Catherine Larouche)*

Bark

Northern white-cedar bark, like the bark of many trees, changes in color and texture as the tree ages, and also varies somewhat with the speed of a tree's growth and its exposure to weather. On saplings, bark is relatively smooth and brown or reddish-brown, but most trees with a trunk more than about 3 inches (8 cm) thick (and quite often smaller than that if they are growing slowly) will develop a pale gray-colored bark, which divides into thin vertical fibers, easily pulled from the tree. In larger diameters, these vertical strips develop into defined ridges that crisscross each other, often following a spiral around the trunk.

Reproductive Structures

As a conifer, northern white-cedar bears no flowers and no fruit. It does produce pollen in spring, and pollinated cones mature in the fall. The mature cones are small (about a half-inch or 1.3 cm long and half as wide), woody, and teardrop shaped, sitting mostly upright on the twigs, often in clusters. Cones are green before they ripen, yellowing to a light brown before they open, spreading out four cone scales to release eight seeds (two per scale). The cones will often remain on the tree for another year after seed release, gradually weathering to a gray color. The seeds are small and flat, oval shaped, about the size of a flake of paprika. The seed itself is just the dark center of the oval; the paler sides are wings to help the seed travel farther in wind.

Wood

"Cedar" is one of the most frequent common names among trees throughout the world, applied to a host of different species in entirely unrelated families. The one thing all "cedars" have in common is a light-weight, aromatic wood. Northern white-cedar fits that description well; it has a distinct, pleasant odor and one of the lightest woods grown by any North American tree. Northern white-cedar wood has a density of about 22 lbs per cubic foot (0.35 grams per cubic cm), compared to eastern hemlock at 28 lbs per cubic foot (0.45 grams per cubic cm) or yellow birch at about 43 lbs per cubic foot (0.69 grams per cubic cm). The heartwood is brown to reddish-brown, distinct from the pale sapwood, but by no means dark. The wood is usually very easy to split, though often revealing a spiral grain. Most of the wood sold in North America as "cedar," outside of local markets, is from western redcedar, northern white-cedar's giant West Coast sibling. The wood is similar.

Form

Northern white-cedar is rarely a large tree, and almost never a tall one; even on the unusual site where it may exceed 60 feet (18 m), its neighbors will be taller still. Its stem often tapers markedly from base to tip, more than almost any other as-sociated tree, except its two family members. This effect is often accen-tuated by broad buttressing at the very base of the tree, especially on wetter sites. Northern white-cedar often have foliage very low down the trunk, frequently within reach of the ground. This occurs with other shade-tolerant conifers such as east-ern hemlock, but does not occur with the other two scale-leaved east-ern conifer trees.

Northern white-cedar tree (*center*) in a forest.

Seedlings

Newly germinated northern white-cedars do not look like adult trees; this is common with many tree species. The first leaves produced by a germinating northern white-cedar are called *cotyledons*—they are preformed within the seed itself, and they consist of one pair of flat, flipper-like needles that are the first green part of a newborn tree. Between this pair, the baby northern white-cedar will next produce a stem covered in "primary" leaves. These are short, flat needles sticking out from the tiny stem in all directions, and the tree will produce only these at first. Over the coming months, or as much as a year or two if growing slowly, the tree will gradually produce more and more of the adult scale-leaves, until it ceases to produce any more primary needles.

Northern white-cedar seedling.

Other Species and Cultivars

Atlantic white-cedar and eastern redcedar occur naturally within parts of northern white-cedar's range, the former just along the Atlantic coast, within a hundred or so miles of the ocean. Eastern redcedar overlaps northern white-cedar at the southern margins of the latter's Midwestern range, in the Appalachian Mountains, in western New York and parts of New England, and extensively in southern Ontario. No other native species are mistakable beyond casual or distant observation, but in developed areas, more possibilities do exist for confusion. There are several Cypress family members that are commonly grown as ornamentals within northern white-cedar's natural or planted range. Most of these are close relatives of either Atlantic white-cedar or eastern redcedar, and will differ in roughly the same ways outlined below for those two. There are three additional species sometimes planted as ornamentals in the east, all superficially similar in foliage and bark:

Species	Distinctions from northern white-cedar
Atlantic white-cedar	spherical, bluish cones much smaller; twigs round in cross-section rather than flat
eastern redcedar	twigs branch three-dimensionally, not in flat sprays; cones are spherical, blue and fleshy, do not open; wood deep red, heavier
Alaska-cedar	drooping foliar sprays (though may resemble some northern white-cedar cultivars); cones small spheres taking two years to mature
Oriental-arborvitae	cones with hooked scale ends; seeds large and wingless; will not survive within most of northern white-cedar's natural range, but both may be planted farther south
western redcedar	cones with six scales, each scale tipped with a small lump or bur that is not present on northern white-cedar

Northern white-cedar comes in a tremendous range of cultivated varieties ("cultivars"), including miniature shrubs, weeping habits, narrow columns, or bearing their foliar sprays in rigidly vertical alignment. Many of these tame cultivars would not survive in the wild, but they do enliven and enrich yards and neighborhoods all across the country.

CHAPTER 2

Traditional and Contemporary Uses:
Northern White-Cedar in Our Lives

There is no doubt that people have played an important role in the events that led to the distribution and amount of northern white-cedar today. That was not always the case. Climate, soils, topography, and natural processes shaped the forests of the upper Great Lakes region, northeastern United States, and southeastern Canada before Europeans arrived. Scattered or small patches of trees died from insects, diseases, and old age, or were blown over by wind, creating openings in the forest canopy. Natural disturbances that killed all the trees across large areas—like catastrophic windstorms or fires caused by lightning—were rare. Indigenous peoples living in those regions cut trees for fuelwood and shelter, and set fires to clear brush for travel and hunting (Stearns 1997). Yet their impacts on the forest were limited relative to those of later European settlers. They hunted white-tailed deer and beaver, a practice that may have locally reduced browsing and flooding of forested wetlands. Some Indigenous peoples cleared upland forests to build settlements and grow crops, but those activities were far less pervasive than they became after European settlement.

Small-scale natural disturbances kill one or a few trees, creating gaps in the canopy.

Northern White-Cedar in the Lives of Indigenous Peoples

North America was populated by an estimated 1 to 6 million Indigenous people between the 1500s and 1700s, when Europeans were exploring and moving to the continent (Milner and Chaplin 2010). Within northern white-cedar's range, populations of Indigenous people were largest in the eastern Great Lakes region (Milner and Chaplin 2010). Starting in the 1600s, Europeans pushed eastern tribes westward. Over the following centuries, repressive colonial policies and outbreaks of infectious diseases such as influenza, measles, and smallpox decimated Indigenous people, reducing populations in some areas by as much as 95% (Stearns 1997). Many Indigenous practices were outlawed, and forest management changed dramatically, with important implications for northern white-cedar populations.

Yet northern white-cedar was and still is integral to the spiritual, ceremonial, medicinal, and material aspects of Indigenous peoples' lives. Many consider this tree sacred and a gift to humanity. Some, including the Ojibwe, place northern white-cedar boughs in their dwellings to protect them from harm (Densmore 1974). Many different Indigenous peoples are familiar with the medicinal properties of northern white-cedar and use the foliage to make warm, moist bandages or preparations (poultices) to ease pain from rheumatism and burns, and tea to relieve constipation and headaches. They have made cough medicine from a concoction of leaves and inner bark, and historically used the vitamin-rich foliage to treat scurvy. It was that use—reportedly shared with Jacques Cartier and his crew by a Haudenosaunee named Domagaia in 1535—that led to northern white-cedar's voyage to Europe and residence in the royal gardens at Fontainebleau (Durzan 2009). Scurvy was a common illness at the time due to poor diet and vitamin C deficiency, and was fatal if left untreated. The miraculous cure Cartier's crew experienced after drinking a decoction of northern white-cedar leaves and bark led them to strip all the branches from a large tree, killing it in less than a week (Moore 1978; Durzan 2009). Beyond the damage done to that one tree, that incident opened northern white-cedar up to new uses by new people. In addition to the name anneda (or hanneda, with various spellings) used by the Haudenosaunee (and giizhik by the Ojibwe, see Sidebar 3), northern white-cedar became known as arborvitae, a European name derived from French and Latin.

Indigenous peoples living within the range of northern white-cedar incorporated items they made from the tree into their everyday lives, with uses varying among tribes according to their needs and resource availability. Members of some tribes insulated their dwellings for the winter by banking the outside walls with northern white-cedar boughs and snow, and filling inside crevices with dried moss. They spread northern white-cedar boughs on the floor and wove mats from strips of bark (Densmore 1974). In the Great Lakes region where wild rice is plentiful, the Ojibwe have long used northern white-cedar wood and bark to make push poles, sticks (knockers), and baskets and bags for gathering and storing rice (Danielsen 2002). They also heat strips of northern white-cedar wood and shape them into wooden frames for snowshoes and sleds. Perhaps the best-known use of northern white-cedar by Indigenous peoples across the region is canoes. Skilled artisans continue this practice today, making canoe ribs, planking, gunnels (gunwales), and thwarts from northern white-cedar.

Indigenous peoples make many small items from northern white-cedar for daily use, including a ring and pin (or bundle and pin) dexterity game. One version played by Ojibwe and Wabanaki people is made by tying a bundle of

SIDEBAR 3 | Cedar Is Ojibwe Life

Christel C. Kern

Northern white-cedar (cedar) embodies all aspects of life past, present, and future for the Ojibwe in northern Wisconsin. Biskakone Greg Johnson, member of the Lac du Flambeau Band of the Lake Superior Chippewa, teaches others about the Ojibwe way of life. In the winter of 2016–2017, he taught me about the exceptional role of cedar in Ojibwe existence.

Biskakone describes cedar through its extensive and deep relationships. From roots to terminal buds, cedar is entirely connected to the land and sky and has a special relationship to water, an element essential to life. This connection to mother earth is a mystery to honor, not to solve.

Biskakone teaching on the Lac du Flambeau Reservation. *(Photo by Carla A. Storm)*

In the forest, cedar has special connections with ash and birch. These connections continue side by side in Ojibwe tools, items, canoes, and homes. In this way, cedar's relationship to other trees extends long after their biological lives in the forest.

Cedar also has a special relationship to people. It is critical to all parts of human existence. In fact, Biskakone described cedar and its relationships in modern-day terms as the hardware store, the department store, the pharmacy, the home, the temple, and so on. It's everything one needs to live.

A single cedar with a straight trunk and diameter greater than 12 inches (30 cm) provides much to the Ojibwe way of life. However, before using any part of cedar, ceremonies are necessary to express gratitude and love to the human relationship with cedar and cedar's relationship to the forest and mother earth. Biskakone emphasized that one must come to the forest in a positive mindset for ceremony and before taking cedar. By doing so, the gifts that cedar provides are useful and with good spirit.

Waakaa'igan. Winter houses are protected by plates of cedar bark. The bark is durable and long-lasting to provide shelter over multiple years. *Cedar provides shelter.* (Photo by Carla A. Storm)

Dikinaagan. Babies are carried in cradle boards that are composed of cedar back and foot boards. The cradle boards are light and sturdy for child care. *Cedar cares for the young.* (Photo by Carla A. Storm)

Jiimaan. Cedar strips, boards, sap, and root twine constitute a large portion of birch bark canoes. The canoes are durable to serve as primary modes of travel, transfer, and fishing. *Cedar gives passage.* (Photo by Carla A. Storm)

Bwaa'iginaatig. Wild rice is knocked from stalks with cedar sticks. The sticks are lightweight to facilitate many days of harvest. *Cedar supports gathering.* (Photo by Carla A. Storm)

Anaakan. Mats woven of inner cedar bark are used to dry fish. The strips are anti-bacterial and anti-fungal, allowing safe food preservation. *Cedar processes food.* (Photo by Carla A. Storm)

Bigiw. Cedar sap serves as medicine. The sap is readily available from live trees all year. *Cedar alleviates sickness.* (Photo by Carla A. Storm)

Left: Bibigwaan. Two pieces of cedar heartwood are carved and joined to create a flute. The instrument produces soothing, melodic tones. *Cedar produces music. Right:* Abaabas. Cedar greens are burned to create smudge used in ceremonies. The greens provide incense and smoke as well and are available all year from live trees. *Cedar expresses customs and prayers. (Photos by Carla A. Storm)*

Biskakone weaving a mat of cedar bark. *(Photo courtesy of Biskakone Greg Johnson)*

A negative mindset affects the tree's spirit such that the subsequent tools, medicines, and other uses are tainted forever and will negatively affect those that use items made of that tree.

Moreover, taking a cedar tree is not a single timber harvest event. The tree parts are gathered in stages. In spring, bark is removed in strips up to 20 feet (6 m) long that could be used for siding and weaving. The tree slowly dies and remains standing in the forest for one or more seasons, still maintaining many relationships with wildlife, the soil, and sky. During this time, greens, sap, and narrow branches from the stripped tree may be gathered for smudges, adhesives, or rice sticks. After death, the tree bole is harvested and cut into boards and strips that may become cradles, canoes, or flutes. Lastly, in time, the gatherer will come back for the roots to make twine. Nothing from a cedar tree goes to waste.

The most important message I learned from Biskakone is that cedar is connected to people in tangible, obvious ways such as canoe building, but also in ways unknown and intangible. Cedar is not a product or resource. More simply, as Biskakone told me, "Cedar is life."

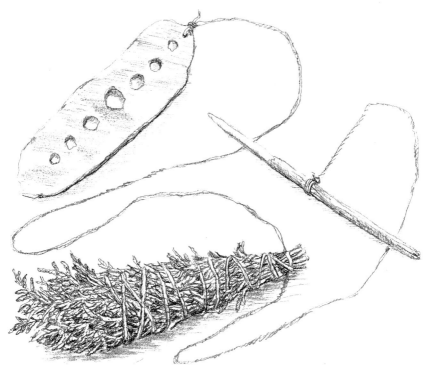

Northern white-cedar bundle and pin game. *(Illustration by Michael A. Klafke)*

northern white-cedar twigs or eastern white pine needles to a carved wooden pin using a string about 6 inches (15 cm) long; some versions include a piece of moose hide with small holes. The object of the game is to toss the bundle and spear it or the moose hide with the pin, earning one point each time (Culin 1907). Other small items made of northern white-cedar include whistles, flutes, tinder (shredded bark for starting fires), and spiles (spigots) to collect sap from sugar maple trees for making syrup and sugar (Densmore 1974). Ojibwe people, for instance, moved each spring from their winter camps to a sugar camp, cut small notches into the trees, and inserted a spile—often carved from northern white-cedar and about 6 inches (15 cm) long and 2 inches (5 cm) wide with a curved surface underneath—to funnel the dripping sap into a container (usually made of birch bark) on the ground below (Marrone 2009; Minnesota Historical Society 2021). Ojibwe people continue this tradition today.

Northern white-cedar spiles used to collect sap for making maple syrup.
(Illustration by Michael A. Klafke)

European Settlers' Uses of Northern White-Cedar

Until the mid to late 1700s, most French and English immigrants to North America were exploring and engaging in missionary efforts and fur trading (Stearns 1997). Their populations were low, particularly in the Great Lakes region, and their impacts on forests were often similar to those of Indigenous peoples. By the 1800s, however, European settlers' activities were causing unprecedented changes to northern forests. At that time, the federal government made large amounts of land available to them for farming and logging, accelerating land clearing (Horwitz 1980). By the mid 1800s, lumbermen in the northeastern United States and Atlantic provinces of Canada realized that supplies of desired timber such as eastern white pine were becoming scarce and profits were dwindling. They looked westward to meet the ever-growing demand for timber, extending railroads into the northern forest to transport wood to mills. Northern white-cedar, though susceptible to decay when living, is highly resistant to decay after death. This is likely because it contains compounds that are toxic to fungi and bacteria that invade dead trees, but not to those that invade living trees (R. Rice, pers. comm., 26 April 2010). Because northern white-cedar wood was both decay-resistant and readily available, many trees of this species were harvested for use as railroad ties and corduroy roads (made by laying logs perpendicular to the direction of the road in swampy areas). Corduroy roads, named after corduroy fabric because of their ridged surface, are still used today for logging roads and walking trails. Though notoriously uncomfortable for travelers, these roads can last for centuries; construction workers in the United States and Canada have recently unearthed a number of them built in the 1800s.

Corduroy road. (Illustration by Michael A. Klafke)

In addition to expanding the area from which they harvested, lumbermen switched their primary focus from eastern white pine to hardwoods (e.g., sugar maple, yellow birch, white and black ash, American basswood, and American elm) and other conifers (e.g., northern white-cedar, eastern hemlock, spruce, and balsam fir) to meet demand for specific types of wood for flooring, furniture, barrels, and other products (Flader 1983). In the northern Great Lakes region, loggers cut large amounts of northern white-cedar to be sawn into boards for use as planks and in construction of wells and cisterns (Sandberg 1983). In the northeastern United States and southeastern Canada, many northern white-cedar trees were felled and used to make shingles for roofs of homes and barns (see Sidebar 4). Northern white-cedar shingles are lightweight and easy to make with simple tools. Shingles were an important source of cash income for people living in rural areas; historians found records from 1865 in northern Maine showing that a single landowner produced and sold more than 2 million northern white-cedar shingles in one year (Wood 1935; Judd 1989).

Northern White-Cedar in the Modern Age

Northern white-cedar continued to make important contributions to forest, farm, and urban economies in the early 1900s. Loggers cut the trees for fence posts and telephone poles, mine timbers, and railroad ties. In fact, they continued to harvest this species after the large logging companies slowed sawmill operations and removed rails from the last of the big logging areas in the Great Lakes region. Aldo Leopold, who is renowned for his writing about American forests and conservation, wrote about logging in the Flambeau River region of Wisconsin at that time:

> Like a coyote rummaging in the offal of a deserted camp, the post-logging economy of the Flambeau subsists on the leavings of its own past. "Gypo" pulpwood cutters nose around in the slashings for the occasional small hemlock overlooked in the main logging. A portable sawmill crew dredges the riverbed for sunken "deadheads," many of which drowned during the hell-for-leather log-drives of the glory days. Rows of these mud-stained corpses are drawn up on shore at the old landings—all in perfect condition, and some of great value, for no such pine exists in the north woods today. Post and pole cutters strip the swamps of white cedar; the deer follow them around and strip the felled tops of their foliage. Everybody and everything subsists on leavings. (Leopold 1949)

SIDEBAR 4 Northern White-Cedar Shingles—Past, Present, and Future

Charles Tardif

Past and Present

The wood shingles used by early European immigrants in North America, which we now call *shakes*, were like those that date back to early European history. Colonists in southeastern Canada and New England used shakes to cover roofs of churches, houses, barns, and sheds starting in the middle of the seventeenth century. Production was labor-intensive. Shakes were split from bolts instead of sawn, thicker than modern-day shingles, and more irregular in shape and appearance. In traditional practice, people felled northern white-cedar trees, cut them into 16- to 18-inch (40- to 46-cm) bolts, and then into quarters. They then split the shakes from each quarter parallel to the grain using a mallet and froe (a tool with a blade at a right angle to the handle). They smoothed and tapered the split pieces on a shaving horse using a draw knife. When finished, they had a flat shake about 1/2 to 7/8 inches (1 to 2 cm) thick, 3 to 8 inches (7 to 20 cm) wide, and 14 to 36 inches (36 to 91 cm) long.

Traditional shingle production using a mallet and froe (*right*) and draw knife (*left*). (*Illustration by Michael A. Klafke*)

Shingle production with a circular saw of the type used in the late nineteenth century and twentieth century.

Though shakes are still made from western redcedar using machines, they are no longer produced commercially from northern white-cedar. The northern white-cedar trees in today's second-growth forests (those that originated after earlier cutting) are smaller than those in colonial times. The trees today are more suitable for shingle production, because shingles are smaller than shakes and are sawn instead of split. Companies began mass production of northern white-cedar shingles in the eastern United States and Canada when circular saws were introduced into mills in the 1800s. The standard procedure in the shingle mill was for workers to divide the logs into bolts, then place a bolt on the carriage of the sawing machine. The carriage (a moveable frame that held the wood in place) enabled the saw operator to tilt and push the bolt through the saw to slice off one shingle with each cut; the carriage automatically moved back to repeat the cutting process until the maximum number of tapered shingles was sliced from each bolt. Workers then used a smaller saw, called an *edger*, to remove waste wood and square the sides of the shingle before sending it to the packer to bundle the shingles. The process for making shingles has remained largely unchanged to the present day, though safety guards have been added to the saws to protect the operator from harm, and modern motorization and sawing tools have been adopted.

Even though the market for cedar shingles has been around for a long time, it remains strong on the East Coast, especially in New England. People living in areas such as Cape Cod, Martha's Vineyard, and Nantucket

Island often cover their homes with natural or stained shingles in various colors, finishes, and shapes. These shingles are made mostly from northern white-cedar but sometimes from western redcedar. The western redcedar trees used for shingles come primarily from British Columbia and to a lesser proportion from the Pacific Northwest states. They are larger than northern white-cedar trees harvested for shingle production in the east. Though it is easier to find clear (knot-free) wood for higher-grade (better quality, #1 perfection grade) shingles from larger western redcedar trees, tannins in western redcedar may cause discoloration when treated with opaque stain. Shingles made from western redcedar are thus more suitable for semitranslucent stains, or if an oil-based primer is applied before the opaque stain finish. Northern white-cedar tends to yield smaller clears (pieces of knot-free wood, grades A and B), but is more suitable for opaque stains. Many people also prefer natural unstained shingles. There is space in the market for shingles of both species, offering a wide range of architectural design options.

Modern-day saw for shingle production and finished shingles.

Future

Predicting the future use of northern white-cedar trees for shingle production in eastern North America requires an understanding of a number of economic and cultural issues. Foremost among these is the availability and sustainability of the northern white-cedar resource in eastern Canada, the Lake States, and New England. Other factors include consumers' changing preferences with regard to shingle color and shape, quality, ease of installation, cost, and whether the product is environmentally friendly.

Despite competition from other products mimicking wood appearance (vinyl, plastic, aluminum, wood composite, etc.), northern white-cedar shingles remain the high-end product of choice for customers willing to pay a premium for highly aesthetic and durable wood. Yet, production is limited by availability of quality wood. This trend is expected to continue in the future as the large trees needed to manufacture high-grade shingles become scarcer. Producers are already finding increased market acceptance of shingles with knots. New approaches to manufacturing quality shingles from smaller trees will probably be necessary in the future—for instance, jointed, glued, and engineered shingles.

In addition to resource constraints, the viability of the cedar shingle industry is affected by political and economic factors. The Great Recession of 2007 to 2009, for example, significantly affected the structure of the shingle industry. Profitability and access to markets are also influenced by United States–Canada trade policies. In addition to the shingle industry—which uses the largest share of the northern white-cedar resource—some large and many small family-owned companies use this species to manufacture furniture, fences, log homes, and gardening products. For all of these companies producing northern white-cedar products, increased innovation, mechanization, and automation will be required to remain viable and competitive in the future.

Leopold's colorful language reflects the reality that most forests of the north-eastern and north-central United States had been cut over—stripped of large trees and desired species—by the early 1900s. Loggers removed first pine, then spruce, then other conifers and hardwoods, leaving fewer species and smaller trees with each pass. This was a time when logging was big business in the northern forest with both "company men" working for industry and "gypo loggers" working as contractors or independent operators. The name *gypo* (or *gyppo*), which may have been derived from the word *gypsy*, was used by unions to disparage independent operators (Mittleman 1923). In fact, these independent loggers were second- or third-generation descendants of early European settlers who have been described as "the most colorful and independent workers in American industry" (Williamson 1976). They commuted daily with their rubber-tired trucks to the winter woods to cut and haul trees to mills to earn much-needed revenue to supplement income on subsistence family farms (Gerald L. Storm, author of this book, is the descendent of independent loggers who cut northern white-cedar in Wisconsin).

Bundling shingles at a sawmill in the early twentieth century. *(Illustration by Michael A. Klafke)*

Cutting northern white-cedar trees for posts, poles, and ties in the 1920s: skidding a log and a pile of posts with tools. *(Illustrations by Michael A. Klafke)*

During the 1930s, 1940s, and early 1950s, stands of spruce and balsam fir were attractive to independent loggers for their value as pulpwood, and northern white-cedar for posts and poles. During a three-month winter harvest in the 1940s in northern Wisconsin, for example, a two- to three-person crew could cut and remove between 1,000 and 1,500 northern white-cedar trees along with several cords (one cord = 128 cubic feet, or 4 cubic meters) of spruce and balsam fir from a 20-acre (8-ha) lowland stand. They cut the spruce and balsam fir into 8-foot (2.4-meter) bolts and delivered them to pulp or paper mills, and cut the northern white-cedar into poles to hold yard lights and telephone lines, fence posts, and posts that held shades for American ginseng gardens (Pinkerton 1947). Telephone companies used about 40 poles per mile (25 per kilometer) for telephone lines, while farmers used about 700 posts per mile (440 per kilometer) for fencing on a typical 80- to 120-acre (32- to 48-hectare) dairy farm (Hoover 1991). According to former loggers, dairy farmers in that region during the late 1940s and early 1950s paid about $75 to $90 for a truckload of three hundred posts: 25 cents for each split post and 30 cents for each round (unsplit) post.

Truckload of northern white-cedar posts delivered to a dairy farm in Wisconsin in the 1940s.

John Curtis (1959), a well-known professor of botany, described the effects of harvesting for these uses in Wisconsin in the mid 1900s and noted the lack of silviculture (the art and science of sustainably managing forests):

> Currently the northern lowland forests are used largely as sources of wood products. White cedar is the main species, with a relatively constant demand for fence posts, fence pickets, and other uses where its superior decay resistance is of value. Black spruce is used as a source of paper pulp in areas where extensive stands are present. Both the cedar and spruce are selectively cut, with little or no attention to the silvicultural needs of these or other species. In general, the northern swamps are not managed, but are merely tolerated and exploited for what they will produce.

Northern White-Cedar Today

Northern white-cedar posts, cut into 6.5-foot (2-meter) lengths, were used on farms for wood and barbed-wire fences until the mid-twentieth century. By that time farmers had replaced most of the wooden fences with metal rods, porcelain insulators, and electric wire that became the primary fence system in rural areas to manage livestock in pastures and outdoor holding pens. Nevertheless, northern white-cedar is still used for fence posts today, though pine and other species treated with creosote, pentachlorophenol, or chromated copper arsenate as well as posts made of steel are more common. Some northern white-cedar trees are used for constructing split-rail fences in fields and pastures, and for preserving historic landscapes in national parks and historic sites. You can build a simple stacked split-rail fence without any nails or other hardware, and without post holes. Simply lay down a rail, then place the next at an angle, on top of the end of the first; these are also sometimes called *zigzag fences* because of their pattern. Another version, called a *cow high and hog tight fence* because it was both high enough for cows and tight enough for hogs, consists of fieldstone overlaid by a series of paired rails, each pair forming a cross that supports rails laid horizontally above the stone.

Just as northern white-cedar fence posts were largely replaced by steel, the iconic canoe with frames and ribs of northern white-cedar has evolved into a modern version. Today's canoes are still lightweight and sleek but may not feature northern white-cedar components. Yet northern white-cedar is still considered one of the best raw materials for making key components of canoes.

Stacked (zigzag) split-rail fence, and cow high and hog tight fence. *(Illustrations by Michael A. Klafke)*

Northern white-cedar footbridge in Acadia National Park, Maine.

Similarly, logs of this species are often used for walking trails and bridges in recreation areas for the same reasons they were once commonly used to make corduroy roads: they are durable and rot-resistant. Northern white-cedar trees also continue to be a preferred source of wood for log homes and specialty products, such as pails, flower boxes, furniture, and storage and hope chests. Though less common today than they once were, you can find cedar chests in most furniture stores in a variety of handcrafted styles, including some made from hand-peeled logs to complement rustic cabin furniture.

Many homeowners in New England and along the eastern coast of the United States prefer northern white-cedar shingles for their homes and barns. Wooden shingle production has become highly mechanized, and the harvesting and processing of northern white-cedar for the shingle market is a multimillion-dollar industry supporting rural economies and sectors of forest industry (see Sidebar 4). Northern white-cedar is also among species such as red pine, eastern white pine, white spruce, and western redcedar used for constructing log homes and cabins throughout North America. In addition to being naturally resistant to insect infestations and decay, northern white-cedar wood has a cell structure that traps air to boost insulation values and shrinks less than other species used in log home construction.

Cordwood homes are also made of northern white-cedar and are arguably more unique than log homes. Cordwood construction (also called *stackwall* or *stovewood construction*) is a building technique developed in North America in

Contemporary northern white-cedar log home exterior and interior. *(Photos courtesy of Katahdin Cedar Log Homes, Oakfield, Maine)*

the mid-1800s that can use wood from curved, crooked, and hollow conifers, including northern white-cedar. Richard Flatau, a leading cordwood builder and teacher, explained to us that the walls are made by embedding 16-inch (41-cm) pieces of wood between two 3-inch (8-cm) mortar beads and filling the empty spaces with insulation such as sawdust and planer shavings. The builder places the pieces of wood in the mortar matrix, one row at a time, and the mortar is finished with a 1-inch (2.5-cm) joint (tuck-pointed) to ensure proper bonding. The long-term durability of the cordwood wall lies in the function of the wood's longitudinal fibers that act like tiny vessels to transfer moisture to the surrounding atmosphere. A post and beam frame supports the roof. If the roof stays in good repair and water is directed away from the bottom log ends, the breathability of a cordwood wall enables it to transpire moisture and stay dry. This allows the untreated and unsealed log ends to last for many years. Cordwood construction lends itself to using imperfect wood, recycling, and artistic displays, and is promoted as a type of planet-friendly construction.

Finally, the twenty-first-century cedar product that has probably reached the most lives is garden mulch. Made by chipping the portions of northern white-cedar trees that are too small, too deformed, or too decayed for other uses, mulch is used commercially and residentially to hold moisture, reduce weeds, and improve garden aesthetics. It may be dyed black, brown, or red, or sold in its natural state. Mulch actually doesn't generate enough profit to cover harvesting and production costs, but it generates additional income for mill owners when made as a byproduct of shingle, post, or other manufacture. On one hand, it is sad that most people's most intimate experience with this patient, persistent, and resourceful tree is to plunge their gloved hands into a plastic bag of colored chips. On the other hand, spreading tiny pieces of northern white-cedar around flowering plants and shrubs, where they slowly decay and return to the soil, seems an appropriate if oddly funereal end to the tree's life.

In fact, northern white-cedar remains sacred to many Indigenous peoples just as it was hundreds of years ago, and practitioners of homeopathic medicine use it in various compounds to treat a range of health woes. And it was surprising, when telling people we were writing a book about northern white-cedar, how many said, "I love northern-white cedar!" or "I have northern white-cedar shingles on my house." Though most of us in twenty-first-century society have distanced ourselves from the way of life that brought our ancestors into close daily contact with, and cultivated deep appreciation for, northern white-cedar, the memory of that connection is still

Cordwood construction: building a cordwood wall (*left*) and a cordwood building (the Cordwood Education Center) in Wisconsin (*above*).

(*Photos by Richard Flatau*)

with us. And yet we have, through industrialization and mechanization, accelerated the rate at which we can use the resource. We have also—by eliminating predators such as mountain lions and gray wolves, clearing land and then abandoning it, intermixing open spaces and forests, and asking policymakers and resource managers to help us see more deer—increased deer populations to densities much higher than they would otherwise be encountered. We have created through both our actions and our indifference a threat to the sustainability of northern white-cedar, while harvesting only a small portion of the wood that grows each year. How can that be possible? It suggests that preservation is not the only answer, for it does not solve the problem of too few successful northern white-cedar offspring. We will need wise policymaking and stewardship of plant and animal populations to get back on track.

CHAPTER 3

Geographic Distribution: Space and Time

Before exploring options for sustaining northern white-cedar, we will consider where it is found, how it got there, and what the future holds. The
geographic area across which a species is naturally found is its native range. For
better or worse, many species of plants and animals live outside their native
ranges thanks to the interference of humans. In some cases, the introduction
of a species from one region to another has disastrous results. In North America, a number of plants brought from Europe or Asia for use as ornamentals
or livestock forage proliferated, invading natural habitats and outcompeting
native plants. Northern white-cedar traveled the other way, carried by New
World explorers back to Europe. Unlike some of its more unruly nonnative
invasive neighbors here in the United States and Canada (for example, glossy
buckthorn, purple loosestrife, and nonnative Phragmites and reed canarygrass)
(Lukkarinen 2014; Smith 2017; New York Natural Heritage Program 2021),
northern white-cedar seems to have behaved well in places where it was planted
by people. Today, there are many cultivated varieties (cultivars) of northern

Cultivated northern white-cedar. *(Photo by Richard Kenefic)*

white-cedar not only in the United States and Canada, but throughout Europe and as far away as China (Bai et al. 2020). Both cultivated and native northern white-cedar are widely available for purchase and can tolerate the climates of most of the United States and Canada south of the Yukon, Northwest Territories, and Nunavut, though some cultivars are less cold-tolerant than others. A planted northern white-cedar might provide you an opportunity to enjoy this species if you don't have access to these trees in forests; hedges of northern white-cedar are often used in landscaping as privacy screens.

Native northern white-cedar in forests of the United States and Canada are integral to the health and function of the plant and animal communities in which they grow. In order to understand those relationships, we must first understand where northern white-cedar grows and why. At the largest scale is its range. Within that range, some but not all habitats are suitable for northern white-cedar, depending on abiotic factors (nonliving components of the ecosystem) such as soil fertility and water availability. Within those habitats where it is capable of growing, its presence and abundance are further influenced by biotic factors (related to living components of the ecosystem) such as competition from other species, browsing by white-tailed deer or other wildlife, and use or overuse by humans. All of these things—range, habitats, and communities—can change over time.

Historical Perspective

Taking the long view, most of the places where northern white-cedar grows naturally today were covered by ice up to two miles (3 km) thick during the last glacial period, before the ice receded from the region between 16,000 and 10,000 years ago (Dyke and Prest 1987). That is equivalent to the height of more than eight Empire State Buildings stacked on top of one another. At that time, the Laurentide Ice Sheet covered North America as far south as present-day Iowa and northern Pennsylvania. Plants that lived out the ice age in southern refugia began to move northward relatively soon after the glaciers started to melt. By studying fossils of pollen and other plant material, scientists estimate that northern white-cedar reached lowland forests in present-day Minnesota about 10,000 years ago and Ontario 2,500 years after that (Janssen 1968; Yu 1997). Northward migration was somewhat earlier in New England and Atlantic Canada, with relatively rapid (in geologic time) forest development about 11,000 years ago (Davis and Jacobson 1985).

Today, the native range of northern white-cedar extends from Manitoba to Nova Scotia in Canada and from Minnesota to Maine in the United States, with isolated populations reported as far south as the Appalachian Mountains of West Virginia, Virginia, North Carolina, and Tennessee. It is common in some parts of its range; recent inventories of number of merchantable-size trees—those with stems at least 5 inches (12.7 cm) in diameter at chest height—show that it is ranked the third-most abundant tree in Michigan, fourth-most abundant tree in Maine and Minnesota, and sixth-most abundant tree in Wisconsin (USDA Forest Service 2018, 2019). Yet northern white-cedar is rare in other parts of its range. It is currently state-listed as threatened in Kentucky, Maryland, and Connecticut, and endangered in Indiana, New Jersey, and Massachusetts (Connecticut DEEP 2015; New Jersey DPF 2016; Office of Kentucky Natural Preserves 2019; Indiana DNR 2020; Massachusetts DFW 2020; Maryland DNR 2021). It is also considered an imperiled species in West Virginia and a vulnerable species in Nova Scotia (Nova Scotia

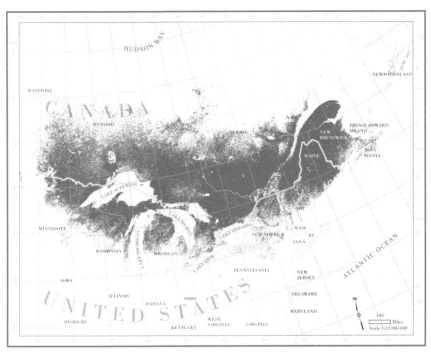

The current distribution of northern white-cedar (map by Claude Dufour, Cedar Club). Forest inventory data from Canada (Beaudoin et al. 2017), and the United States (Wilson et al. 2013) were used to determine presence or absence of northern white-cedar in pixels 820 by 820 feet (250 by 250 meters). Pixels with at least one northern white-cedar at the time of inventory are shown in gray.

DNR 2010; West Virginia DNR 2020). This variability in abundance is due to a number of factors, among them regional variation in patterns of precipitation and temperature. Though climate across the region is relatively humid, average annual precipitation varies from about 28 to 46 inches (71 to 117 cm) but can be as much as 55 inches (140 cm) at the southern extent or as little as 20 inches (51 cm) at the northern and western extents. Mean annual temperature varies from less than 50° F (10° C) in the Great Lakes region to 60° F (16° C) in the Appalachians, with about 165 days with below-freezing temperatures at its southern extent in the United States and 285 days at its northern extent in Canada (Johnston 1990).

If planted northern white-cedar can grow outside its range, why aren't northern white-cedar forests more widespread? The reasons are related not only to climate, but natural disturbances and human land use. The western boundary of northern white-cedar's range falls along prairie grasslands where fire and insufficient moisture keep forests from expanding westward (Greller 2000; Heinrichs 2009). These factors, as well as our use of the land for agriculture, restrict expansion of northern white-cedar in western Minnesota (Zenner and Almendinger 2012). In addition to agriculture, urban development prevents northern white-cedar from expanding south of its current range in Wisconsin and Michigan (Radeloff et al. 2005; Rhemtulla et al. 2009). At its northern range limit, scientists suspect disturbances such as wildfire limit its northward expansion (Jules et al. 2018; Rayfield et al. 2021). In isolated southern populations, high temperatures during the growing season seem to limit northern white-cedar's growth (Kincaid 2017).

Yet we should not view northern white-cedar's range as fixed in time. In the context of the earth's history, the thousands of years northern white-cedar has occupied its current range are merely a short visit. Likewise, colonization of the northern forest by trees after the last ice age was rapid in geologic time, though it took a few thousand years. The rate and success of each species' range expansion was and will continue to be influenced by factors including the conditions required by the seeds for germination and likelihood of dispersal by wind or animals. Most northern white-cedar trees don't reliably produce seeds until they are close to thirty years old, with best production after seventy-five years, and the seeds are usually carried by wind for less than 100 feet (30 m) in forest stands (Johnston 1990; Cornett et al. 1997). In comparison, paper birch—a tree that often grows with northern white-cedar—produces seeds at about half that age that travel more than twice as far (Safford et al. 1990).

Wherever northern white-cedar seeds fall, they require certain conditions for germination. On drier sites, the seeds need substrates that hold moisture, like exposed mineral soil or decayed logs, to germinate and survive. On wetter sites, too much water can be a problem. Here, regeneration from seeds is most successful on elevated microsites—such as those formed by buried wood—that provide refuge from seasonal flooding. In fact, the primary means of northern white-cedar regeneration on lowlands where soils are saturated is not from seeds, but from layers: stems and branches that grow roots when resting on the ground, ultimately growing into new trees that can survive on their own (see Sidebar 5). Though this adaptation helps northern white-cedar thrive in habitats that are too wet for other species, it restricts regeneration to the area reached by branches or stems of the parent tree.

Left: Northern white-cedar seedlings growing on a decayed stump. *Right:* A line of northern white-cedar trees that likely grew from the layered branches of a fallen tree.

Recent Trends

Though northern white-cedar trees were used by many Indigenous peoples in North America, we now know that their impacts on the species' population were far less than those of European settlers. Widespread land clearing and intensive harvesting didn't start until Europeans came to the New World. We don't know the exact distribution and abundance of northern white-cedar in North America before European settlers arrived, but scientists have made estimates from historical records and early land surveys. All of them concluded that large areas of northern white-cedar forestland have been lost, both in the United States and in Canada. In southern Quebec, for instance, northern white-cedar has declined by 12% since the 1800s, with the greatest losses in areas where people harvested intensively or cleared land (Danneyrolles et al. 2017). Even greater reductions have occurred in the Lake States. In Minnesota, the area of northern white-cedar forest is now half what it once was, again due to harvesting and land clearing (Cornett et al. 2000; Zenner and Almendinger 2012). In northern Wisconsin, the reduction is estimated to be 75% (Habeck and Curtis 1959).

SIDEBAR 5 | Reproduction by Layering

Jay Wason

One of the most vulnerable times in a plant's life is when it first emerges from a seed. A seed is simply a partially developed tree seedling enclosed in a protective seed coat with a small supply of food. For northern white-cedar, seeds have small wings that aid with long-distance dispersal by the wind to a suitable location for germination and growth. As a northern white-cedar seed germinates, the partially developed tree seedling emerges, sending leaves up to capture light and roots down to capture moisture and nutrients. This is an extremely vulnerable time for the tree seedling, and most tree seedlings in nature do not survive long past this stage. The benefits of reproduction by seed are numerous, including long-distance dispersal and diversifying the genetics of a population. However, some tree species, like northern white-cedar, have adopted a second form of regeneration that avoids the sensitive life stage following germination.

Northern white-cedar seeds and seedling. *(Illustration by Jeanette Allogio)*

Layering is vegetative reproduction from above-ground stems. When these stems come in contact with a moist substrate, they can develop new roots while still attached to the parent plant. Sometimes that stem with its new root system becomes disconnected from the parent plant, but often they remain connected for many years. Layering is common in wetland trees and can be an excellent way for trees (or gardeners) to quickly create new individuals. Although lacking the benefits of long-distance dispersal and mixing genetics that occur during reproduction by seed, regeneration by layering has its benefits. For example, in comparison to a seedling, a layer can be a robust plant because it starts with a larger shoot system and is often still connected to a parent plant that can supply it with water, nutrients, and energy as it develops. Indeed, we often find that survival of layers is higher than seedlings during stressful conditions.

Layering is often imagined as a large parent tree gracefully bowing a branch to the ground to form roots and new offspring. Although northern white-cedar does layer in this way, we often find much more complex and fascinating examples of the formation of layers. For example, a common type of layering in northern white-cedar swamps appears to be when a small seedling or sapling tree originally grown from seed is completely bent over to the ground (presumably by snow). That small tree then forms new roots along its stem (layering) and shoots continue to develop above. As those shoots get taller, the seedling may be pushed down again, leading to another episode of layering from the shoots that developed after the first layering event. Thus, we often find large patches of northern white-cedar regeneration in the forest that, once carefully excavated, are all connected by stems now buried with moss. Indeed, there are particularly interesting cases of the same seedling being bent in the same direction and repeatedly layering resulting in a long line of regeneration. Careful analysis can help us re-create the history of these groups of regeneration all the way back to the original seedling that emerged from a seed as many as forty years earlier.

We are still learning about the importance of layering as a regeneration pathway for the ecology of northern white-cedar, but a few things are becoming clear. Much, if not most, of the regeneration in some forest stands is created by small trees layering rather than regeneration from seeds. These robust patches of layers all interconnected below ground may actually be a mechanism of long-term persistence of northern

Northern white-cedar can regenerate by layering as roots form from stems in contact with the ground. These layers can come from seedlings (*left*) or tree branches (*right*). If the stem is resting on the ground (*top*), roots can develop (*middle*), and a new individual is formed that can support itself even if the connection to the parent plant is broken (*bottom*).   *(Illustration by Jeanette Allogio)*

white-cedar as they withstand repeated browsing and other pressures. Their shared root systems and distribution of nutrients and energy can be a benefit in this stressful condition. However, like many shade-tolerant trees, northern white-cedar regeneration is patiently waiting for a canopy gap opening to spur new growth. In this new high-light environment, suddenly, a patch of layers all supporting each other during stressful times through below-ground connections become competitors in the race for light and a dominant position in the canopy.

In Nova Scotia, northern white-cedar was reportedly common in the 1600s but reduced to scattered trees in a few stands by the 1980s (Johnson 1986). In his comprehensive report of the forests of Nova Scotia, Ralph Johnson (1986) concluded that its presence in the province at that time was "too small to warrant further discussion."

And yet data from the U.S. Forest Service's inventory of New England and the Lake States (USDA Forest Service 2012) show about 1 billion northern white-cedar trees (what foresters call *growing stock*) at least 5 inches (12.7 cm) in diameter at chest height (USDA Forest Service 2012; see Appendix C). Even at a modest height of 40 feet (12 meters), that's enough northern white-cedar trees to reach to the moon and back more than a dozen times. There is no doubt that is good news, but there are concerns about maintaining this population. Though the amount of northern white-cedar harvested in recent decades is far less than the amount that grew across the region, harvest has exceeded growth in some localities (Hofmeyer et al. 2010). In addition, while the number and volume (amount of wood) of very large northern white-cedar trees (called *sawtimber*) has increased in recent decades, the number of seedlings and saplings has decreased in parts of the Lake States and other places where deer populations are high.

Though northern white-cedar trees can grow quite rapidly on fertile sites if they have access to moisture and are free from competition and browsing—growing more than 1.5 feet (0.5 m) in height per year (Villemaire-Côté et al. 2017)—most trees of this species grow very slowly. Scientists reported that average diameter growth of northern white-cedar trees in New England, Quebec, and the Atlantic provinces is less than 0.1 inch (0.25 cm) per year (Boulfroy et al. 2012). In Maine, it takes 170 years, on average, for a northern white-cedar tree to grow from a seedling 1 foot (0.3 m) tall to a tree large enough to make shingles (10 inches or 25.4 cm in diameter at chest height) (Hofmeyer et al. 2010). In addition, northern white-cedar has a unique adaptation: the internal plumbing (xylem) that carries water and nutrients from its roots to its branches is sectioned so that each branch is supported by a specific root (Larson et al. 1993, 1994). Though this enables a northern white-cedar tree to thrive even when some sections are dead, it prevents it from redistributing resources and thus is an adaptation for survival, not rapid growth. It is clear that northern white-cedar is an aging resource, with old trees getting older and too few young trees, growing too slowly for long-term sustainability of the resource.

A living northern white-cedar tree with a dead section in its main stem.

What's Next?

Today, the earth's climate is changing rapidly due to the warming effects of increased carbon dioxide and other gases in the atmosphere. In addition to warming temperatures, changes in climate alter precipitation patterns and lead to more extreme weather events such as severe storms and periods of drought. A warming climate also reduces snowpack and causes earlier spring thaw (Burakowski et al. 2008), leading to soil freezing, root damage, and reduced nutrient uptake (Sanders-DeMott et al. 2019). This is already negatively affecting trees similar to northern white-cedar. Scientists believe that a decline in Alaska-cedar in the North Pacific Coastal Rainforest of British Columbia and Alaska is due to late-winter and early-spring root freezing caused by reduced snow cover (Hennon et al. 2012).

As a result of these climate changes, environmental conditions in the places where northern white-cedar lives now may become inhospitable for the species. Scientists have already determined that warm temperatures early in the growing season negatively affect growth of northern white-cedar at the southern extent of its range (Kincaid 2017). But environmental changes happening now are happening more quickly than trees generally, and northern white-cedar specifically, can colonize new habitats as they did after the last ice age. Nothing about northern white-cedar's approach to regeneration—its relatively late-in-life start to seed production, seeds that fall near the parent tree, or reliance on layering—suggests rapid range expansion. The image of northern white-cedar slowly crawling northward, one layered branch at a time, is not encouraging.

Over the past century, average annual temperature in the Great Lakes and New England, where northern white-cedar lives, has increased by 1.4° F (0.8° C) (Hayhoe et al. 2007). Over the next century, the expected increase is 2.7° to 8.0° F (1.5° to 4.4° C). Even an increase in the middle of that range (about 4° F, or 2.2° C) is expected to result in deciduous trees replacing conifers throughout much of the northern forest (Davis 1990). In the Boundary Waters region of northern Minnesota and southwestern Ontario, for example, temperature increases of that magnitude could cause forested wetlands of northern white-cedar to become treeless sedge and grass meadows (Heinselman 1996).

Overall, climate change effects on lowland conifer forests are expected to vary across the region, but are generally neutral to negative (Handler et al. 2014a, 2014b; Janowiak et al. 2014, 2018). Northern white-cedar has been characterized as a climate change "loser" with projected declines in suitable

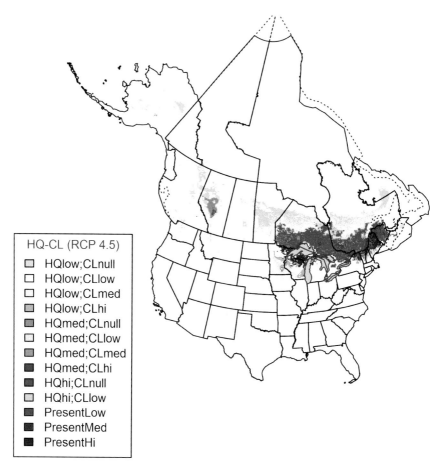

Current (present) and predicted future (year 2100) northern white-cedar habitat under the climate change scenario associated with intermediate concentrations of greenhouse gases (representative concentration pathway or RCP of 4.5). Habitat quality (HQ) and natural colonization likelihood (CL) are categorized as low, medium (med), or high (hi), with different colors and shades for various combinations of HQ and CL (CLnull indicates no probability of natural colonization) (Prasad et al. 2020a, 2020b).

habitat, tree numbers, and biomass due to death of existing trees and regeneration failures (Iverson et al. 2008; Handler et al. 2014a, 2014b; Janowiak et al. 2014, 2018). Particular concerns related to northern white-cedar include effects of hydrologic changes on regeneration substrates and early growth, the possibility of increased browsing by deer due to range shifts and reduced

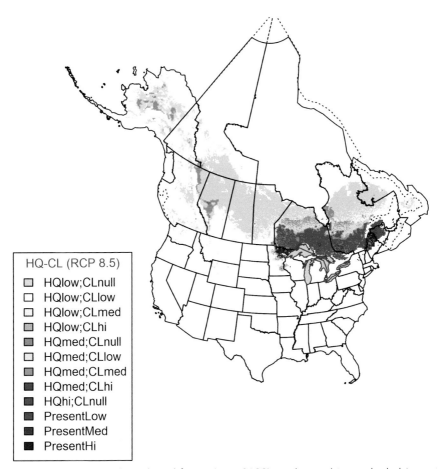

Current (present) and predicted future (year 2100) northern white-cedar habitat under the climate change scenario associated with high concentrations of greenhouse gases (RCP of 8.5). (Prasad et al. 2020a, 2020b).

snow cover, and declines in abundance over the long term if existing trees die and new trees fail to grow because habitats have become unsuitable. If current trends in greenhouse gas emissions continue, researchers predict that northern white-cedar will be extirpated (locally extinct) from parts of its current range before the end of the twenty-first century (Janowiak et al. 2018).

CHAPTER 4

Natural Communities: Friends and Neighbors

In light of concerns about the future of northern white-cedar, it is important to fully understand its current distribution and abundance, evaluate its ecological and social importance, and develop a strategy for conservation and sustainable use. In the previous chapter, we discussed the range of northern white-cedar and how that has changed and will continue to change over time. But knowing the extent of northern white-cedar's range and whether it is expanding or contracting isn't enough to understand what is happening to the species. We must also know why these changes are occurring, and for that we must know the characteristics of the places where northern white-cedar lives and the assemblages of plants and animals there. This will help us understand the many connections between northern white-cedar trees and their communities, an important first step in devising a plan to ensure that they continue to thrive.

One of the many values of northern white-cedar is its contribution to biodiversity. This species lives in diverse habitats and contributes to many assemblages of plants and animals—these are its natural communities. If you look at

Northern white-cedar on lowlands on commercial forestland in Maine (*top*), and on uplands on provincial forestland in Quebec (*bottom*). *(Quebec photo by Catherine Larouche)*

the map of northern white-cedar's range in the previous chapter, you can see that it covers a broad geographic area encompassing different climates, elevations, topographies, and soils. In fact, northern white-cedar grows naturally in swamps, lower slopes and valleys, along lakeshores and streams, and on abandoned pastureland, sandstone bluffs, and limestone cliffs. Each of those habitats supports different natural communities. Just as we recognize people and places in our daily lives, we can recognize not only individual species of plants but the communities in which they live. When we do, we can better understand our natural environment and the importance of habitats and communities to conserving specific organisms.

Landscape Diversity

At the large scale, northern white-cedar lives in many different habitats across the landscape at elevations from near sea level to more than 2,000 feet (610 m) (Grotte 2007). Soils—which determine rooting depth, fertility, and water availability—are a critical component of a tree's habitat and can vary greatly from one location to another. The soils supporting northern white-cedar include well-decomposed plant material (organic matter) near streams, thick mineral soil over sediments (till) deposited by glaciers during the last ice age, thin mineral soil over bedrock outcrops around lakes, and pockets of partially decomposed organic matter (duff) in crevices on cliffs and bluffs (Johnston 1990; Minnesota Department of Natural Resources 2003; Gawler and Cutko 2010; Cohen et al. 2015). Despite their differences, all of these soils have one thing in common: they provide northern white-cedar with reliable access to moisture.

Just like soils, assemblages of plants and animals differ among northern white-cedar's natural communities. Scientists have classified and named these communities to bring order to what would otherwise be a dizzying array of species in various combinations across sites. Yet because classification and naming systems have been developed separately by each state and province, it can be difficult to understand how communities in one place relate to those in another. For that reason, broad categories based on some overarching feature can be useful for splitting or lumping natural community types. For northern white-cedar, scientists often make this distinction based on whether a community is found in a lowland or upland habitat.

Lowlands, as the word suggests, are relatively low-lying areas in floodplains, along streams, and on adjacent lands formed by similar geologic processes.

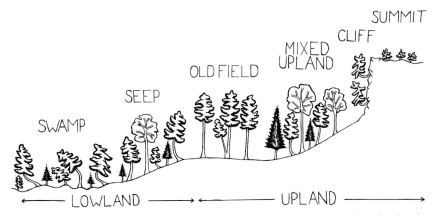

A schematic showing northern white-cedar communities in lowland and upland landscape positions. *(Illustration by Jeanette Allogio)*

Uplands are on comparatively higher ground, usually above the floodplain and the gentle slopes at the bottoms of hills. Northern white-cedar grows fastest on uplands with moist, well-drained, calcium-rich soils derived from limestone, but tends to be more dominant on lowlands with organic soils. It flourishes in large numbers in forested wetlands (swamps) and seeps near lakes and streams where groundwater flows below or rises to the surface. Scientists think that northern white-cedar is more abundant on these sites because it faces less competition and damaging fires are infrequent (Johnston 1980; Johnston and Booker 1983).

Even though northern white-cedar swamps are a common natural community type, trees in swamps tend to grow slowly and can be prone to decay (Fowells 1965). Scientists have observed that northern white-cedar trees grow more rapidly and have less decay on uplands where soils are better drained, with moving groundwater rich in oxygen and nutrients (Pregitzer 1991; Hofmeyer et al. 2009; Kell 2009). On abandoned pastureland in New England and southern Quebec, for example, stands of what is known as *old-field* northern white-cedar tend to be fast-growing with good form and little decay (Curtis 1946). Such stands are a legacy of our use of the land rather than natural processes alone. Cattle browse less heavily on northern white-cedar than its competitors, and northern white-cedar seedlings are able to withstand trampling (de Blois and Bouchard 1995). For these reasons, northern white-cedar trees grow well on pastureland, albeit often

An old-field northern white-cedar stand in Vermont where local farmers cut small trees to use as fence posts.

with multiple stems. Local farmers cut these trees to use as fence posts; it is common to see barbed wire on locally sourced northern white-cedar posts around fields in northern Vermont and elsewhere.

Natural Communities

Natural communities—groups of interacting plants and animals and their physical environment—result from natural processes rather than human activities. They might occur repeatedly across the landscape where environmental conditions are similar. Identifying and naming natural communities helps us make sense of natural variation (Gawler and Cutko 2010) and is a necessary first step in developing plans for conservation or restoration. Because trees are larger and live longer than most other plants, they have an outsized effect on the characteristics of a natural community. Similarly, among the tree species in a community—which may be few or many—those that are most abundant

Examples of some natural community types with northern white-cedar:

(a) *Forested Seep*, Flambeau River State Forest, Wisconsin. *(Photo by Susanne von Schroeder)*
(b) *Rich Conifer Swamp*, Dukes Experimental Forest, Michigan.
(c) Volcanic Cliff, Porcupine Mountains Wilderness State Park, Michigan. *(Photo by Friedrich Wendorff)*
(d) *Evergreen Seepage Forest*, Penobscot Experimental Forest, Maine.
(e) *Northern Wet-Mesic Forest*, Argonne Experimental Forest, Wisconsin.
(f) *Rocky Summit Heath*, Cadillac Mountain, Maine.

(called the *dominant tree species*) tend to have the greatest influence. If management is desired and feasible, it would logically be driven in large part by the characteristics of those species. For this reason, our focus here is on communities in which northern white-cedar is dominant, though it is common throughout its range in communities where other species predominate, and contributes importantly to biodiversity there too. After narrowing our focus to the communities where northern white-cedar is dominant, we find that there are relatively few, even in the four states where it is most abundant: Minnesota, Michigan, Wisconsin, and Maine. Natural community types similar to these are also found in Canada; examples from Quebec are described in Sidebar 6.

Lowland Communities

Forested wetland community types where northern white-cedar is a dominant species include White Cedar Swamp in Minnesota, Rich Conifer Swamp in Michigan, Northern Wet-Mesic Forest in Wisconsin, and Northern White Cedar Swamp in Maine, among others (Minnesota Department of Natural Resources 2003; Gawler and Cutko 2010; Cohen et al. 2015; Epstein 2017). Soils are typically organic and include deep, saturated peat (partially decomposed plant material), muck (well-decomposed plant matter), and shallow peat over mineral soil. Though the water table remains at or near the surface for much of the year, northern white-cedar swamps have moving groundwater rich in nutrients and oxygen that allows diverse plant communities to flourish. The forest floor is a lush carpet of bryophytes such as sphagnum and brown mosses. Keeping company with the northern white-cedar are a number of conifers and hardwoods, including varying amounts of black, white, and (in Maine) red spruce; tamarack; balsam fir; eastern white pine; black ash; red maple; and birch and aspen species. Species of alder, honeysuckle, holly, raspberry, and blueberry are among the shrubs often found in these swamps. The diverse non-woody plants include a number of rare or otherwise sensitive plants such as fairy slipper (calypso orchid), ram's head lady's slipper, showy lady's slipper, and roundleaf orchid (Gawler and Cutko 2010; Epstein 2017; see Appendix D). In fact, in the Great Lakes region several rare plant species occur more frequently in northern white-cedar swamps than in any other habitat (Epstein et al. 2002). This association of northern white-cedar with rare plants is an excellent example of why it's important to conserve natural communities, rather than focus only on charismatic animals or plants.

Rare orchids found
in northern white-
cedar swamps
include the fairy
slipper (*above
left*), ram's head
lady's slipper
(*above right*), and
roundleaf orchid
(*left*). *(Photos by
Chelsea Kieffer)*

SIDEBAR 6   Natural Community Types in Quebec

Guy Lessard, Catherine Larouche, and Emmanuelle Boulfroy

Northern white-cedar is found on about 15% of the forest land in its natural range in Quebec. It occurs most commonly as a minor species (< 25% of stand composition) with other softwoods such as balsam fir and black, red, and white spruce, and with hardwoods such as yellow birch and black ash. Northern white-cedar occurs as the dominant species (> 50% of stand composition) in some stands.

In Quebec, natural community types are represented by different species assemblages, associated with varying characteristics of topography, drainage, moisture, and soils. Shrub and herbaceous species beneath the tree canopy also help define these different community types. They inform forest management, support long-term inventory and monitoring efforts related to biodiversity, and help natural resource managers assess the welfare of native plant communities. The different natural community types associated with northern white-cedar are described here as lowlands and uplands.

Lowlands

In the lowlands of Quebec, northern white-cedar may be the dominant tree species in two types: (1) Cedar and (2) Balsam Fir and Cedar, which occur on moist deep mineral soils or very moist deep mineral or organic soils. Companion tree species are balsam fir; black, red, and white spruce; and paper birch. Speckled alder, cinnamon fern, and sphagnum moss help indicate the Cedar type. Mountain maple, beaked hazel, American fly honeysuckle, dwarf red blackberry, long beech fern, and speckled alder help indicate the Balsam Fir and Cedar type.

Northern white-cedar may also be part of the Yellow Birch and Balsam Fir type and the Black Ash and Balsam Fir type. These two types, allied with very moist deep mineral or organic soils, may be found with tree assemblages consisting of balsam fir, black ash, quaking aspen, yellow and paper birch, and red maple. The Yellow Birch and Balsam Fir type is also recognized by mountain maple, woodfern, wild sarsaparilla, beaked hazel, and American fly honeysuckle. Black ash, speckled alder, cinnamon fern, graminaceous plants, sedge (*Carex*), heartleaf foamflower, and sensitive fern help identify the Black Ash and Balsam Fir type.

Examples of lowland (*top*) and upland (*bottom*) natural communities with northern white-cedar in Quebec. *(Photos by Guy Lessard)*

Uplands

Northern white-cedar occurs on uplands in Quebec on very thin soil or out-crops, or dry to moderately dry deep soils. Although northern white-cedar is not a common dominant species on moderately dry or moist soils, it is frequently present as a companion species in the Yellow Birch and Balsam Fir type and Balsam Fir and Cedar type. It is not uncommon to find paper birch, sugar maple, and red maple along with yellow birch, balsam fir, and northern white-cedar. Mountain woodsorrel, mountain-ash, threeleaf goldthread, Indian-cucumber, hairy Solomon's seal, false Solomon's seal, and Canada yew may help indicate those community types.

In southern Quebec, northern white-cedar may also be the dominant tree species on abandoned farmlands (old fields and pastures). Such stands are included in the community type Balsam Fir, White Birch, and/or Cedar associated with agricultural sites with deep, fine-textured dry or moist soils.

Thus, four types of natural communities of northern white-cedar stand out: (1) Cedar and (2) Balsam Fir and Cedar in uplands and (3) Yellow Birch and Balsam Fir and (4) Balsam Fir and Cedar in lowlands. Each has its own dynamics, issues, and potentials for forest management.

Northern white-cedar swamps have unusually high structural diversity, which helps to diversify habitat. Many birds, mammals, insects, and fungi rely on structures in forests that look messy to people, like broken branches, dead treetops, leaning or fallen trees, and damaged or hollow stems. Because of their shallow roots, northern white-cedar trees in swamps sometimes fall over during wind or ice storms, creating pits and mounds on the forest floor and tangles of leaning stems and branches that shelter many species of wildlife. Wind and ice cause branches to break, and falling trees or logging machinery can damage stems and roots, allowing fungi to colonize living trees. Insects and woodpeckers excavate the exposed wood, creating cavities for nesting. Wildlife need many of these small habitat features (microhabitats) to feed, shelter, or breed at some point in their lives (Larrieu et al. 2018).

Northern white-cedar can be a dominant species in lowland seepage forests on gentle lower slopes or near lakes and streams where groundwater rises to the surface. These natural community types, such as the Lowland White Cedar Forest in Minnesota and Evergreen Seepage Forest in Maine, are often slightly upslope from those in swamps (Minnesota Department of Natural Resources 2003; Gawler and Cutko 2010). Underlying soils are typically shallow peat or muck over mineral soil, or mucky mineral soil (mineral soil with a high proportion of well-decomposed organic matter). As you might guess from those descriptions, these soils tend to be saturated with groundwater, which sometimes emerges in spring-fed brooks. On the forest floor, feather mosses and liverworts are more abundant than sphagnum (peat) moss. Intermixed with northern white-cedar trees are varying numbers of black, white, and (in Maine) red spruce, as well as balsam fir, black ash, red maple, and paper, yellow, or mountain paper birch depending on region and site. Shrubs such as American fly honeysuckle, mountain maple, and speckled alder are present but tend to be less abundant than in northern white-cedar swamps. Both upland and wetland species of herbaceous plants grow here, sometimes including the rare orchids showy lady's slipper and giant rattlesnake-plantain, the latter of which is threatened in some areas by collecting and logging (Gawler and Cutko 2010; Maine Department of Agriculture, Conservation and Forestry 2015).

Upland Communities

Natural community types on uplands where northern white-cedar is a dominant tree species include White Cedar–Yellow Birch Forest in Minnesota, Boreal Forest in Michigan and Wisconsin, and White Cedar Woodland in Maine,

◀ Structural complexity in a northern white-cedar stand.

Giant rattlesnake-plantain. *(Photo by Chelsea Kieffer)*

among others (Minnesota Department of Natural Resources 2003; Gawler and Cutko 2010; Cohen et al. 2015; Epstein 2017). You will often find these wooded upland communities on moderate to steep slopes with thin mineral soil over bedrock, though soils and moisture regimes vary. Bryophyte cover ranges from sparse to plentiful depending on community type, but typically includes dicranum and other mosses. Balsam fir or eastern white pine are abundant (Gawler and Cutko 2010; Cohen et al. 2015; Epstein 2017). Other associated tree species in the Lake States include yellow, paper, or mountain paper birch, as well as white spruce in the Boreal Forest community type. The mix of shrubs and non-woody plants depends on how much water is present, but can include various species of honeysuckles, hollies, and blueberries; woodfern; shining clubmoss; and starflower. Rare or otherwise sensitive plants, such as fairy slipper and ram's head lady's slipper, may also grow in these communities (Cohen et al. 2015; Epstein 2017).

Northern white-cedar can also predominate on cliffs and bluffs. In the forested Wet Cliff community type in Wisconsin, northern white-cedar, eastern hemlock, eastern white pine, and balsam fir grow on damp vertical bedrock or eroded bedrock ridges undercut by streams (Epstein 2017). These communities often occur in dense shade on slopes facing north and east, where direct sunlight is limited and conditions are cool and moist. Other woody species growing here include Canada yew, red elderberry, and mountain maple. In the understory, ferns and herbaceous species like bluebell bellflower, orange and yellow jewelweed, wild columbine, and wild sarsaparilla flourish. These difficult-to-access habitats are also home to the rare carnivorous plant common butterwort—which has leaves that excrete a sticky fluid that traps insects to be digested and absorbed by the plant—as well as the threatened northern blue monkshood and the endangered Lapland rosebay (Epstein 2017).

Unlike the Wet Cliff community type in Wisconsin, some cliff and bluff communities have sparse plant cover and stunted trees due to poorly developed soils, erosion, and exposure to the elements. In Michigan, the Clay Bluff natural community type occurs on steep, nearly vertical clay slopes along the shores of Lakes Superior and Michigan (Cohen et al. 2015). Only scattered, stunted northern white-cedar grow there, along with willow, paper birch, as well as jewelweed, alder, dogwood, and cherry species. In Maine, the Rocky Summit Heath natural community type grows on exposed bedrock on upper slopes and ridges near the coast and inland (Gawler and Cutko 2010). Soils consist of a thin layer of organic duff in bedrock pockets. Dwarf shrubs such as lowbush blueberry and northern mountain cranberry grow beneath red and black spruce, balsam fir, and northern white-cedar trees that become patchy and stunted as elevation increases.

Even in seemingly inhospitable environments like cliffs and bluffs, northern white-cedar trees can survive for many hundreds of years. Scientists have found very old trees in the Boundary Waters Canoe Area Wilderness and Great River Bluffs State Park in Minnesota, and on the north shore of Lake Superior and the Niagara Escarpment (Tester 1995; Minnesota Department of Natural Resources 1996, 2005). Stretching from upstate New York, through southern Ontario, and into Michigan, Wisconsin, and Illinois, the Escarpment is home to northern white-cedar trees more than 1,500 years old (Larson and Kelly 1991).

To find out more about all of the natural communities in which northern white-cedar and its neighbors live, consult the many state guides that offer detailed descriptions and useful photographs, species lists, and conservation and management suggestions.

Changes in Natural Communities

The process of change in natural communities after a disturbance—a destructive storm or fire, for example—is known as *succession*. Though scientists have recognized that plant communities change for millennia, the concept of an orderly process of predictable change was not fully developed until the last century. In particular, the work of American ecologist Frederic Clements advanced our understanding of succession and promoted the idea that development after disturbance proceeds in one direction and results in a single, stable community called the *climax community* (Clements 1916; Odum 1969; Leopold et al. 1996). During this process one species or group of species was thought to dominate the community until being replaced by another. Prior to the mid-twentieth century, ecology textbooks generally supported this understanding of succession. In lowland forests, for example, ecologists believed that pioneering communities of sedges and grasses gave way to shrubs such as alder and willow, then to a more permanent, mature tree community (Aaseng et al. 1993). This mature community would experience fewer changes in species composition and structure than had occurred in earlier stages.

Unfortunately, succession is rarely that simple. Many different and competing theories developed, and the topic of succession now occupies multiple chapters in many ecology textbooks. To put it simply, scientists questioned the

Common butterwort. *(Photo by Andreas Fleischmann)*

Mature northern white-cedar, Dukes Experimental Forest, Michigan.

idea that natural communities follow a predictable sequence of change ending in a single, stable climax condition. Instead, they now recognize that—among other complexities—frequent disturbances change the successional pathways in many community types, meaning that progression toward a stable climax might not occur. Fire, windstorms, insect infestations, fungal infections, and nonnative invasive plants are so common that a stable climax community might be the exception rather than the rule (Tester 1995). Today, scientists generally accept that natural communities are in a constant state of change, and most ecosystems do not exhibit a stable endpoint or successional climax condition.

What does this constant state of change look like in northern white-cedar's communities? In forests where it grows, natural disturbances typically create small openings in the canopy. These canopy gaps result from trees dying of old age, windthrow, breakage, or localized insect or disease outbreaks. When a canopy tree dies, the light, water, and nutrients it was using become available to other vegetation. If the gap is small (created by the death of one or a few trees), then branches and roots of existing trees might take up these newly available resources, or seedlings of species tolerant of shade might start to grow in the partially illuminated understory. If the gap is large (created by the death of multiple trees), then species that are intolerant of shade and those that benefit from disturbance, such as paper birch or pin cherry, might grow. In either case, gap dynamics add compositional and structural complexity to an established forest community and are common in northern white-cedar stands (Ruel et al. 2014; Fraver et al. 2020). Northern white-cedar, with its shade tolerance and exceptional longevity, has the ability to not only persevere but thrive in such stands over the very long term.

A number of factors lead to deviations from the expected development of natural communities as described above. Browsing by white-tailed deer, for example, can greatly change community structure and composition, particularly with regard to the amount of northern white-cedar and other plant species they selectively browse. This may account for the many northern-white cedar stands in the Lake States and New England that have understories of balsam fir instead of northern white-cedar (e.g., Johnston 1972; Kenefic et al. 2020). Because northern white-cedar can live hundreds of years longer than balsam fir,

Northern white-cedar stand with an understory of balsam fir near Dismal Swamp in Maine.

we would expect stands composed of these two species to become increasingly dominated by northern white-cedar over time. Yet the young trees growing beneath the canopies of many northern white-cedar stands—the trees poised to capture newly available resources in gaps and ascend to the canopy—are often balsam fir rather than northern white-cedar. Why is this compositional shift happening in two regions a thousand miles apart? Scientists think the driving factor may be excessive browsing by deer, which prefer northern white-cedar foliage to that of balsam fir. Similarly, Canada yew was once a common species throughout much of northern white-cedar's range but has also suffered from deer browsing to the point that it is now scarce or absent from many stands where it once grew (Lemieux 2010).

Effects of Human Disturbances

Deer are not the only ones to blame for declining numbers of northern white-cedar in some parts of its range. People have degraded some of the natural communities in which the tree usually grows, including the globally rare Alvar communities found on the shorelines of the Great Lakes in the United States and Canada. This natural community type occurs on thin soil over bedrock, is prone to wet and dry cycles, and may have open, savanna-like forest cover. Rare plants and animals such as the threatened dwarf lake iris and cherrystone drop land snail live here. Yet quarrying, road construction, and residential development are serious dangers to these unique communities (Epstein 2017). Scientists have cautioned that we must prioritize these areas for protection and restoration.

Some common northern white-cedar communities have also been degraded by people but might respond well to careful management. Roads intercept groundwater near northern white-cedar swamps, causing flooding on one side and drying out (dewatering) on the other (Chimner et al. 2017). Urban development disrupts the movement of water through the soil, as well as water uptake by plants. Large openings created by some types of harvesting create conditions inhospitable for northern white-cedar, leading to shifts to other tree or shrub species. Other threats include the spread of nonnative invasive plants such as glossy buckthorn and marsh thistle, and as we've already discussed, excessive browsing by deer, particularly in the Lake States (Rooney and Waller 2003). Climate change is likely to exacerbate all of these threats as the conditions northern white-cedar encounters become increasingly different from those to which it is adapted. The ability of the tree to successfully regenerate is of particular concern, as increased variability in precipitation and climate increases the probability that fragile seedlings will succumb to flooding or drought.

In short, many things people do disrupt plant communities, ecosystem stability, and the values ecosystems provide (ecosystem services). These services include not only maintaining biodiversity and producing wood, but recharging groundwater, filtering pollutants, and storing carbon to counteract the effects of greenhouse gas emission and climate change. Better planning, siting, and technological changes can mitigate damage associated with road building and construction (see Sidebar 7). Where northern white-cedar trees are abundant and sites suitable, integrating species' requirements for regeneration and growth into forest management will lead to more favorable outcomes. In all of these instances, careful consideration of the structure and function of natural communities can help guide sustainable use, restoration, or preservation of northern white-cedar and its diverse communities.

CHAPTER 5

Northern White-Cedar and Wildlife: More Friends and Neighbors

There is no doubt that northern white-cedar is important in many natural communities, both as an individual species with inherent ecological and economic value, and as an integral part of relationships and dependencies between plants and animals. From tiny leafminers tunneling inside the foliage to 500-pound (225-kg) male black bears biting and scratching trees during mating season, northern white-cedar is a part of daily life for many organisms living in its communities. Awareness of these interactions is crucial to understanding the role of northern white-cedar in the function and biodiversity of the ecosystems where it lives. To that end, we will take a closer look at some of those living things—small and large—and consider how northern white-cedar helps them flourish and, in return, the impacts they have on the trees.

Fungi and Insects

Most references to fungi and insects in the literature about northern white-cedar focus on those that are detrimental to the tree's vigor or wood soundness and quality. Though the word *fungus* conjures up images of mushrooms and toad-stools, fungi live in many forms throughout forests in the soil, litter layer, dead-wood, and living trees, both seen and unseen. Until recently, scientists thought fungi were plants. This misclassification goes all the way back to Swedish bota-nist Carl Linnaeus in the early 1700s. Though regarded as the father of modern taxonomy (the science of classifying living things), Linnaeus had it wrong with regard to fungi. His distinction was based on his observation that "Vegeta-blia crescunt & vivunt. Animalia crescunt, vivunt & sentiunt."—which means "Plants grow and live. Animals grow, live and feel." (Linnaeus 1735). In fact, fungi are neither plants nor animals. Unlike plants, they do not photosynthe-size and thus cannot make their own food. Unlike animals, they do not ingest food; they absorb it from their environment (Lovett 2021). Fungi with unflat-tering names like white stringy rot and brown cubical rot are well known to for-esters for colonizing trees through damaged roots and stems, then decaying the wood by excreting enzymes that break down cellulose and starch and convert them into sugars. Yet of the many fungi living in northern white-cedar commu-nities, most are benign or beneficial from the trees' perspective. Mycorrhizae are particularly important within the group of organisms northern white-cedar calls friends. Mycorrhizae are symbiotic associations between fungi and tree roots. Fungal mycelia (thread-like structures) spread over long distances in the soil, absorbing water and nutrients and transporting them to the trees' roots. In return the fungi absorb sugars from the trees. Some mycorrhizae are added to soils in nurseries to help seedlings grow. In fact, scientists have observed that inoculating peatland soils with certain types of mycorrhizae has the same effect on northern white-cedar growth as adding fertilizer (Anwar et al. 2020).

Just like fungi, there are innumerable insects living in northern white-cedar communities, most not affecting the tree but benefiting from the microhabi-tats provided by loose bark, exposed wood, branches, foliage, deadwood, and cavities. Those of concern to foresters damage wood soundness (like carpenter ants that colonize trees after fungal infection) or reduce tree vigor. Insects that consume living foliage (called *defoliators*), for example, limit a tree's ability to photosynthesize, starving it of the energy it needs to grow. A tree that has lost too much foliage over too long a period of time may die. One such insect that poses a threat to northern white-cedar is the arborvitae leafminer. This tiny moth with a wingspan of less than 0.3 inch (8 mm) lays its eggs on northern white-cedar's scale-like needles. When the larvae hatch they tunnel directly into the foliage, eating it from the inside out and causing it to brown and die.

Arborvitae leafminer moth. *(Photo by Petr Kapitola, Central Institute for Supervising and Testing in Agriculture, Bugwood.org)*

Foresters in Maine, Quebec, and New Brunswick reported a number of years in which northern white-cedar foliage turned brown in the mid-twentieth century, sometimes killing trees (Nutting 1949; Silver 1957; Bazinet and Sears 1979; Natural Resources Canada 2015). In fact, scientists studying tree rings—the lines created in cross sections of tree stems when growth ceases at the end of each growing season—have observed that northern white-cedar trees grew very little in some parts of Maine at times when arborvitae leafminer populations were high. Though not previously thought to be a problem in the Lake States, an outbreak of arborvitae leafminer was detected in Minnesota in 2017, causing defoliation of northern white-cedar across thousands of acres of forestland (Minnesota Department of Natural Resources 2019).

Also of recent concern, a nonnative Japanese cedar longhorn beetle was accidentally introduced to the United States in wood imported from Asia, and has been damaging northern white-cedar and junipers in some parts of the Northeast since the early 2000s (Maier 2007). This insect is not yet widespread, and infestation of live northern white-cedar trees is primarily restricted to those from nurseries that are already stressed by poor growing conditions. The beetle seems to prefer dead northern white-cedar with bark. Overall, though injuries caused by some fungi and insects reduce the commercial value of northern white-cedar trees and result in periods of slow growth or even mortality, there are none known to threaten the survival of trees across whole stands or regions at this time.

Birds and Mammals

The illustrations in the following pages were painted for us by Wisconsin artist Michael A. Klafke to show some of the birds and mammals you might find in northern white-cedar stands. Of these, snowshoe hare and white-tailed deer are arguably the most consistent users of northern white-cedar for food and shelter across the region, especially for thermal cover in winter. While some of the species shown here have little effect on northern white-cedar, others use the species to its detriment. This is certainly true of snowshoe hare and deer; both can cause northern white-cedar regeneration or recruitment failures where the animals' populations are high (seedlings start to grow but are killed or become stunted by repeated browsing). Unlike the lowly mycorrhizae bringing nutrients to its roots and red squirrels inadvertently dispersing seeds while running off with clipped branchlets in their mouths, many of northern white-cedar's animal neighbors are more "frenemies" than friends. And yet, that is the fate of trees in forests. By virtue of living such outsized lives—bigger and longer than others in their communities—they end up giving a little or a lot to keep the community as a whole thriving.

In the Air

Wildlife biologists have observed more than forty species of birds in northern white-cedar forests in Michigan, including ruffed and spruce grouse, common redpolls, slate-colored juncos, tree sparrows, and fifteen species of warblers, among others (Doepker and Ozoga 1991). Male ruffed grouse often use northern white-cedar lowlands during the breeding season. They perch on a downed log and make a deep thumping sound (drumming) by swiftly rotating their wings forward and backward to both attract females and warn off other males. Yet while the drumming sound can be heard up to a quarter-mile away, the bird's cryptic (camouflage) coloring makes it difficult to see in northern white-cedar swamps.

Other birds that live among northern white-cedar include the pine siskin (which is particularly fond of northern white-cedar seeds) and pileated, black-backed, and three-toed woodpeckers. Pileated woodpeckers, up to 19 inches (49 cm) long with a wingspan of 2.5 feet (0.8 m), are the largest woodpeckers in northern forests. These woodpeckers use their feet (which have two toes facing forward and two toes facing backward) to grip the trunks of trees and brace themselves with their tail feathers while excavating wood to find insects.

Ruffed grouse. *(Illustration by Michael A. Klafke)*

They use their chisel-shaped bill to create oblong openings for feeding and round holes for nesting; the tip regrows over time, similar to our fingernails. The woodpecker's tongue is twice as long as its bill and has a barbed tip covered with sticky mucus that helps it reach insects deep in chambers in dead wood.

Beneath the Canopy

In addition to the many birds that northern white-cedar calls friends and neighbors, there are just as many mammals, frogs, salamanders, and turtles in their communities (Doepker and Ozoga 1991). Northern flying squirrels glide through the forest canopy and gather northern white-cedar bark for their nests. In a hardwood forest in southern Ontario, for instance, cavity nesting material used by flying squirrels consisted almost entirely of shredded bark from northern white-cedar. One female flying squirrel traveled more than 1,640 feet (500 m) to the nearest northern white-cedar tree to gather bark for her nest (Patterson et al. 2007). Scientists think this is a behavioral adaptation the squirrels developed

Pileated woodpeckers. *(Illustration by Michael A. Klafke)*

because—like cedar chests and closets—nests made of northern white-cedar keep insects away.

Red squirrels, chipmunks, voles, and mice feed on northern white-cedar cones, while numerous species eat northern white-cedar foliage. Though foraging by large mammals can kill regeneration of northern white-cedar, the

Flying squirrel. *(Illustration by Michael A. Klafke)*

intensity of the effect depends on the type of animal is doing the feeding. In Wisconsin and Michigan, for example, elk frequently browse northern white-cedar and will select it for food even when quantities are limited (Moran 1973; Lizotte 1998). Moose, on the other hand, tend to eat northern white-cedar

Snowshoe hare (*bottom right*) and bobcat. *(Illustration by Michael A. Klafke)*

only when other preferred foods are not available, despite the fact that they often shelter in lowland northern white-cedar stands (Eastman 1995; Tester 1995). Snowshoe hare and deer, however, consistently use northern white-cedar for food and shelter; both species have been blamed for regeneration and recruitment failures in the Lake States and New England (Aldous 1941; Nelson 1951; Alverson et al. 1988). Though deer are notorious browsers of northern white-cedar, snowshoe hare damage northern white-cedar regeneration as much as or more than deer in some locales (Fowells 1965). Snowshoe hare are unusual among northern forest animals in that their reddish-brown coats become white in winter, helping them hide from predators such as bobcats, coyotes, and hawks. Just as climate change is expected to make some habitats unsuitable for northern white-cedar, longer periods without snow during mild winters could make snowshoe hares wearing white winter coats more vulnerable to predation (Burt et al. 2017).

White-tailed deer. *(Illustration by Michael A. Klafke)*

Though deer do not change color, they have adapted to cold conditions by developing a much thicker winter coat and moving around less and more slowly to conserve energy (Moen 1973). Nevertheless, chances of winter survival are greater if deer can find dense stands of northern white-cedar or other conifers to protect them from deep snow and wind. Their overwinter survival is further improved if northern white-cedar foliage is available for food. Unfortunately, overabundant deer populations can strip all the foliage within reach, killing small trees and causing northern white-cedar regeneration or recruitment to fail. This threatens future habitat availability because there aren't enough young cedar trees to replace those in the overstory that die in stands with many deer: a classic case of biting (or in this case, completely consuming) the hand that feeds you.

Another large northern forest animal, the black bear, doesn't eat northern white-cedar foliage but does strip the bark to chew off the sugar-rich sapwood underneath when food is scarce in the early spring (Nolte et al. 2003). A single bear can strip as many as seventy trees in a day, damaging and sometimes killing them. Bears also claw or rub against the rough bark of northern white-cedar trees to communicate with one another during mating season; you might find tufts of fur caught in the bark. Other aspects of bears' relationships with northern white-cedar are less stressful for the trees. Bears have been known to bed down with their bellies in the cool, mossy carpet of northern white-cedar swamps on hot summer days. This bear equivalent of a spa day coincides with bears' annual molt when their bellies are sparsely covered with fur. Also in the summer, young cubs may take refuge high up in large northern white-cedar or eastern white pine trees to avoid adult males during breeding season. They grasp the rough bark with their curved claws and footpads and squeeze the trunk with their arms and legs as they scramble up to their lookouts.

Another charismatic species associated with northern white-cedar swamps—beaver—does not prefer northern white-cedar for food (Müller-Schwarze 2011). Yet beavers build dams that flood lowlands, killing northern white-cedar trees and other plants. Beavers have been called *ecosystem engineers*: they create and maintain habitats for other species. In fact, though beaver ponds and lodges are remarkable habitats that support many species, they change the natural flow of water in ways that benefit some communities but disadvantage others. Beavers themselves are endowed with special attributes to live in the ponds they create behind their dams. They can close their nostrils and throat while swimming and carrying branches in the water, and they have a thin membrane over their eyes that protects them from injury and allows them to see underwater. Their fur coat and oil glands reduce heat loss in cold, wet environments. Northern white-cedar is not so lucky. Though the trees can tolerate seasonal high water, they cannot live with their roots completely submerged for long periods of time. A conspicuous outcome of beaver activity is mortality of northern white-cedar and other trees in flooded forests.

Returning Our Focus to the Trees

One of the threads running through this book—like the threads of fungi running through forest soils—is that all living things are connected in ways that are both seen and unseen. We have a tendency to focus on people first and

Black bears. *(Illustration by Michael A. Klafke)*

Beaver. *(Illustration by Michael A. Klafke)*

charismatic animals second. In addition to our animal-centric view—called *plant blindness* (Wandersee and Schussler 2001)—it has been suggested that people fail to see living things that are not "animals with eyes like ours and backbones" (Knapp 2019). As a result, the more conspicuous animals in our environment attract our attention and concern to the detriment of others. As we consider the interconnectedness that pervades natural communities, balancing the needs of the organisms that we know and love best with those that are unknown to us will remain a challenge. Learning more about northern white-cedar and its natural communities is integral to more informed decision making and management. Past failures in this regard—conspicuously related to deer browsing—highlight the need for continued learning.

CHAPTER 6

White-Tailed Deer and Northern White-Cedar: Biting the Hand That Feeds You

To help understand how things went wrong in the relations between people, white-tailed deer, and northern white-cedar, we invited Keith R. McCaffery, retired deer research biologist with the Wisconsin Department of Natural Resources, to coauthor this chapter with us. The following summary draws upon his expertise and ours, taking into account both historical context and current natural resource management challenges.

For a full understanding of the issue, we need to go back to just before Europeans arrived in the northern forest. Scientists estimate that fall populations of deer were at most—and possibly fewer than—10 to 15 per square mile (about 4 to 6 per square km) in the range of northern white-cedar at that time (Dahlberg and Guettinger 1956; Mattfeld 1984; McCabe and McCabe 1984). Since then, deer populations have fluctuated widely, due in large part to changes in land use, forest composition and structure, predator populations, and hunting. All were caused directly or indirectly by European settlers and their descendants.

Early European explorers and settlers in North America desired deer meat (venison) and hides not just for their own use but to ship to Europe to sell. Killing deer to trade or sell (market hunting) became widespread, causing the deer population to drop to less than half of pre-European-settlement levels by 1800 (McCabe and McCabe 1984). With the exception of a slight increase in deer populations in the early to mid-1800s due to the opening of the forest by logging, the number of deer continued to trend downward and reached unprecedented lows in the late 1800s to early 1900s depending on region. At that time—in what historians now refer to as the exploitation era in the history of white-tailed deer—the number of people living in the United States and Canada was rapidly increasing, and railroads were being built across the northern forest. Market hunters killed and shipped huge numbers of deer (often measured in hundreds of tons) from across northern white-cedar's range, drastically reducing population size (Storm and Palmer 1995; McCabe and McCabe 1984). (The coauthor of this chapter, Keith R. McCaffery, is the great-grandson of a market hunter in Wisconsin who supplied deer to railroad builders and markets in big cities in the 1870s.) Michigan's deer population, for example, was reduced to fewer than 100,000. While this was a hard time to be a deer, it was a good time to be a northern white-cedar. Without browsing by deer, northern white-cedar flourished (Bourdo 1983; Heitzman et al. 1997).

That respite didn't last. Public concern over dwindling deer populations led state and federal governments to enact and enforce laws to curb wholesale slaughter of deer for profit (McCabe and McCabe 1984). Wisconsin's annual bag limit (the number of deer one hunter could kill each year) went from unlimited to two deer in 1897 and then to one deer in 1909. Restricted bag limits, refuges, and shorter hunting seasons fostered herd growth. Important predators such as mountain lions and gray wolves, which hunters had long been paid to kill to protect livestock, had been eliminated from much of the northern forest region. At the same time, intensive logging and land clearing reduced the area of mature forests and increased the area of young forests composed of small trees and rich, sunlit understories; these provided abundant food for deer (McCaffery 1986; Rooney 2001; Waller 2008). Intermixed forests and farms provided food and shelter for deer in close proximity. All of these factors led to a remarkable increase in number of deer.

As deer populations increased, so did their browsing on northern white-cedar. Deer prefer northern white-cedar over other plants available in the winter because it is easy to digest and more nutritious than other winter browse.

White-tailed deer browsing on northern white-cedar.

Dense stands of northern white-cedar provide excellent shelter by intercepting snow and wind. This led many deer to gather in stands where northern white-cedar trees were abundant, concentrating their feeding where proportions of small northern white-cedar were high. As a result, many northern white-cedar stands started to show what is called a *browse line*. This is a line that marks the height reached by deer feeding in winter. In 1907, for instance, an article in a hunting magazine reported that "Along the shores of any of the backwoods ponds of Maine where cedar grows down to the water's edge can be seen a line on the foliage some five feet above water. It has the appearance at a distance of being a high-water mark, or a line caused by deep snow in winter" (Stanton 1963). In fact, all the seedlings, saplings, and lower branches of northern white-cedar trees below the browse line had been eaten by deer.

The science of wildlife management was in its infancy before World War II, and natural resource managers did not have a good understanding of the concept of carrying capacity (the number of individuals of a species an ecosystem can support). Though appropriate deer densities for maintaining healthy deer and plant communities vary across habitats and over time, many wildlife ecologists today put that number at fewer than 10 or 20 per square mile (about 4 or 7 per square km) (deCalesta 2017). Yet by the early 1940s, the number

Northern white-cedar trees with a browse line in Porcupine Mountains Wilderness State Park, Michigan. *(Photo by R. G. Eckstein)*

of deer counted on deer drives in northern Michigan and Wisconsin often exceeded 50 per square mile (19 per square km), sometimes even surpassing 120 per square mile (45 per square km) (Swift 1946). Deer were packed so tightly into lowland stands during winter that nine out of ten fawns (deer less than one year old) died of starvation in some years. In the early 1950s, Michigan, Minnesota, and Wisconsin each reported annual winter mortality of 20,000 to 60,000 deer. To reduce mortality of deer during winter food shortages, state agency personnel and volunteers cut northern white-cedar, mountain maple, willow, and cherry—in addition to supplementing with hay—to provide forage (Dahlberg and Guettinger 1956). Today, wildlife ecologists caution that deer should not be given food because this not only maintains more animals than the ecosystem can support and leads to habitat degradation, but increases the risk of disease-spread among animals that have gathered closely together at feeding stations.

What Went Wrong?

Though the public was rightly concerned about the death of deer, they tended to attribute this to severe winter weather or predation without considering the effects of overpopulation. People generally failed to see (and still fail to see) the damage done by high populations of herbivores to plants in forests. Scientists came up with a term—plant blindness (Wandersee and Schussler 2001)—to describe our inability to see or notice the plants in our environment. Plant blindness prevents us from recognizing the importance of plants in our lives or appreciating their aesthetic and biological features. This can lead us to incorrectly conclude that plants are unworthy of our consideration. This perceived unworthiness is exacerbated in the case of northern white-cedar and deer by the deer's status as a beloved and highly visible part of our culture. We need only consider the cartoon deer Bambi, orphaned when hunters shot his mother in one of the most distressing acts of villainy in the Disney film oeuvre, to understand why we have so willingly turned a blind eye to deer's overuse of forest vegetation and especially the northern white-cedar resource.

In fact, scientists in the Great Lakes region were concerned about the sustainability of northern white-cedar by the 1940s. In addition to heavy browsing by deer, this tree species was further depleted by logging and fires that started near railroads and in piles of branches (slash) loggers left after hauling tree boles away. Northern white-cedar became rare in some places where it had been common, while some stands had a browse line so high that the deer could no longer reach their food (Aldous 1941). In Maine, northern white-cedar saplings became scarce (Curtis 1946). These problems have persisted to the present day in areas where deer populations are high. Scientists in central Maine recently discovered that the number of northern white-cedar saplings declined in some stands by 80% in the second half of the twentieth century (Larouche et al. 2010). Similar declines have been reported in Michigan and Wisconsin (Botti 1991; Forester et al. 2008).

Deer populations continue to fluctuate over time and space. Nevertheless, the number of deer in some of the Lake States has exceeded one million in most years since 1995. In addition to browse lines and too few northern white-cedar saplings, signs of excessive foraging by deer in northern white-cedar stands include declines in rare and endangered orchids and lilies (Cornett et al. 2001). Despite an abundance of seedlings on the forest floor of some stands, very few if any develop into larger stems (i.e., recruit) in areas

White-tailed deer in a northern white-cedar stand in New York.

with high deer densities (Heitzman et al. 1999). Though foresters have ideas about how to regenerate northern white-cedar and accelerate the growth of small trees, such efforts are likely to fail where deer densities are high. For this reason, management of northern white-cedar must be carried out in concert with management of deer to maintain herds at densities compatible with growth of the plants they prefer to eat.

What this density should be is difficult to discern. Scientists in Wisconsin saw little evidence of browsing on northern white-cedar in the Menominee Indian Reservation in the 1960s when deer density was kept at fewer than 5 per square mile (2 per square km) by year-round subsistence hunting of male and female deer. Yet browse lines began to appear on northern white-cedar when the area temporarily came out of reservation status and the state restricted hunting, and deer densities rose to 15 per square mile (6 per square km).

Similarly, scientists working in Maine and Quebec reported good survival of northern white-cedar seedlings in areas with 3 deer per square mile (1 per square km), but poor survival in areas with 14 to 16 deer per square mile (5 to 6 per square km) (Larouche and Ruel 2015). These observations suggest that deer population numbers suitable for regenerating northern white-cedar are lower than most states seek to maintain in the northern forest. Overwinter deer population density goals in forested parts of Wisconsin, for example, ranged from 10 to 25 per square mile (4 to 10 per square km) between the 1960s and early 2000s depending on the forest composition and carrying capacity of each deer management unit (these units were changed in 2015 to generally follow county boundaries and quantitative goals were discontinued) (Wisconsin DNR n.d.).

State goals are generally set in consultation with the public, including hunters who often advocate for more deer. Seeing deer is the number one determinant of a quality hunt for most hunters, and they see fewer when populations decline. Hunter engagement in deer management is crucial for controlling herds, but it is not clear how best to achieve that if their desired population goals exceed those of natural resource managers. There are other routes that have been explored for controlling deer populations, including programs that chemically or surgically sterilize deer (Boulanger et al. 2012). These are expensive, require a long-term commitment, and are not practical when working with free-ranging deer. Sterilization techniques can work where the deer population is contained or isolated with little immigration from elsewhere. With so many competing interests involved and strong feelings on all sides, natural resource managers, policymakers, and the public will need to come together to establish deer population goals and hunting regulations that account for not only social and economic concerns, but health of natural communities. This process is often quite contentious. Rebuilding deer herds as during the first half of the twentieth century is popular, and controlling (reducing) herds can be very controversial. A wildlife ecologist described some hunters' feelings on the matter by saying, "People who wouldn't be activists about anything else will crawl out of their hospital bed and crawl across broken glass to advocate for more deer" (LaCrosse Tribune 2014). Chapter co-author Keith R. McCaffery explains the Wisconsin situation below.

Northern white-cedar sapling browsed by white-tailed deer. *(Photo by Catherine Larouche)*

A Wisconsin Case Study of Deer Management Challenges

Establishing and implementing annual deer-harvest levels has been controversial. One aspect of this that people often disagree about is the availability of permits and priority to shoot antlerless (mostly female) deer. Wildlife ecologists recognize that controlling the number of female deer is the most effective way to control population size, but hunters often prefer to shoot adult bucks. For example, an irruption in deer numbers in northern Wisconsin to a peak population in the year 2000 was generally attributed to a succession of mild winters, marked increases in hunters and landowners feeding deer, and hunter resistance to harvest prescriptions. A record hunting success rate in that year was favorably viewed by hunters, but impacts of deer on northern forests continued to be of concern to natural resource managers. The deer herd was reduced following 2000 by liberal harvests and winter losses. By 2008 both annual harvest of deer and hunter satisfaction with deer management in northern Wisconsin had declined. In response, the state legislature eliminated several harvest management approaches in 2011, including the "Earn a Buck" program that required hunters in overstocked units to kill an antlerless deer before they could shoot an adult buck. This approach had been demonstrated to be an effective tool for reducing deer populations in areas with excessive deer populations and browsing.

An increase in mortality of juvenile deer in winter and neonates (newborns) in spring in Wisconsin after harsh winter conditions in 2013 and 2014 prompted harvest recommendations aimed at protecting antlerless deer in most northern counties. Prescriptions for low harvests continued in subsequent hunting seasons as responsibility for harvest recommendations was transferred from wildlife ecologists to county-level deer advisory councils in 2015. While on a steep learning curve, a few of the northern councils have sought to maintain responsible deer densities while others have worked to build the herd to unsustainable size. Wildlife ecologists pointed out that hunter concerns were in response to a deer population decline from a level of overabundance in 2000 to a level more compatible with long-term goals for ecological sustainability. It is very likely that contentious issues like these, concerning abundance and effects of deer on plant diversity in northern forests, will continue until society accepts the notion that ecosystem management, which places value on all species, is more desirable than management directed at a single game species. We would be wise to adopt Aldo Leopold's land ethic as written in 1949, expanding our moral obligation beyond people to all parts of natural ecosystems: soil, water, plants, and animals.

CHAPTER 7

Management: Having Our Cake and Eating It Too

The fact that northern white-cedar provides critical winter browse for white-tailed deer but does not regenerate where deer populations are high is not the only conundrum natural resource managers face when working with this tree species. Many aspects of northern white-cedar are seemingly contradictory. It is abundant, but there are concerns about sustainability. It grows in swamps and on cliffs, but dies if there is too much or too little water. It regenerates best in the shade, but grows fastest in the sun. It can grow rapidly into large trees with sound wood, but often grows slowly into medium-size trees with decayed wood. And, in perhaps the greatest quandary of all, we value it as a living tree for habitat and biodiversity, but desire it as wood for products we use. Each of these statements includes facts that are hard to reconcile yet must be accounted for by people deciding whether and how best to manage northern white-cedar. In all of these cases, there is more potential for progress if we view these contradictions from a "yes, and" rather than a "no, but" perspective, though the cognitive dissonance can be jarring. With that as context, it is easy to see that it can be difficult to manage northern white-cedar.

The overriding challenge facing foresters managing northern white-cedar in much of the region today is successfully regenerating and recruiting new trees to replace those that die or are harvested. The theme of that endeavor is patience. Regeneration from seed can be unreliable, and regeneration from layers can be hard to predict. Even if new trees start to grow, they are likely to die if submerged in water or deprived of moisture, surpassed by faster-growing species, or eaten by deer. What does this mean? Should we simply preserve all northern white-cedar? Some public agencies have taken this approach where regeneration or recruitment success is uncertain, but many northern white-cedar stands—and the cover they provide for deer—are getting old. If we don't take steps to regenerate northern white-cedar, will there be young trees to replace their parents in all the places where they grow now?

Mature northern white-cedar stand in Michigan.

Many northern white-cedar communities are not in forests suitable for management, and even among those that are, some should not be managed. These are so special, unique, or sensitive that the things we do would compromise the very attributes we seek to maintain. Yet, there are a billion northern white-cedar trees of merchantable size in New England and the Lake States alone, and it is among the five most abundant tree species in three heavily forested states. In places where northern white-cedar is prolific, there are many opportunities for management. In forests with enough trees to make logging operations feasible, we might use harvesting to meet demand for wood products while creating conditions that will sustain northern white-cedar's many values for the future. While harvesting is common on commercial forestland, many other types of landowners also harvest trees to sell or use. A recent survey of family forest owners in the United States found that close to one-third sold timber from their land and one-half harvested trees for their own use (Butler et al. 2016). This suggests potential for increasing management of northern white-cedar.

Understanding Forest Management

It is useful to start with some perspective on forest management. The millions of acres of forestland within the range of northern white-cedar include properties from less than ten to hundreds of thousands of acres. These include areas with meaningfully different soils, natural community types, and histories of disturbance that are owned or managed by a wide range of public agencies, tribes, corporations, nonprofit organizations, individuals, and families. Each wants different things from their forest, such as providing habitat for wildlife, creating opportunities for recreation, producing wood or non-timber forest products, protecting water, or preserving nature. Given this diversity of forest conditions and desired outcomes, there is no "one size fits all" approach.

Even in the absence of management, forests are always changing. Managing forests—usually but not always by harvesting trees—allows us to direct change in a way that achieves our goals. For northern white-cedar, those goals might be to increase light in the understory for new seedlings, reduce competition among crowded trees, or provide habitat for deer. Finally, before deciding whether or how to harvest, forestland owners and managers must consider not only the trees' financial value but the role they play in the ecosystem and how removing them will affect their natural communities. This consideration is part of sustainable management, which requires us to maintain the integrity of forest ecosystems when using forest resources.

Foresters didn't start thinking about sustainable management of northern white-cedar until the mid-twentieth century. Before that time, people harvested northern white-cedar trees with little consideration for the future. We now know that this reduced the abundance of northern white-cedar in parts of its range. As discussed in previous chapters, this happened because people were harvesting northern white-cedar trees faster than they could grow, other species grew in the place of those that were harvested, or deer or snowshoe hare ate the new seedlings and saplings. Natural resource managers now fear that there are too few young northern white-cedar trees, growing too slowly, to replace older trees that die or will be cut in many parts of its range.

In response to these concerns, scientists used findings from research about northern white-cedar regeneration and growth, as well as observations of outcomes of past harvests, to develop silviculture guides (Miller et al. 1991; Schaffer 1996; Boulfroy et al. 2012). Silviculture, which comes from the Latin word for wood (*silva*) and the French word for cultivation (*culture*), is the art and science of sustainably managing forests. (Laura S. Kenefic, author of this book, is a silviculturist; she studies and applies silviculture.) In the following sections, we review the evolution of northern white-cedar silviculture and how the successes and failures along the way help us understand the path forward for managing this species.

Managing for White-Tailed Deer Habitat

Natural resource managers first tried to manage northern white-cedar in the early 1900s because they wanted to provide winter habitat for deer. At that time, most deer populations were recovering from a half century of exploitation. In order for deer yards to provide habitat for many years, new trees need to grow to replace those that die. With this goal in mind, foresters in the Lake States began trying different approaches to northern white-cedar silviculture. One popular approach was to harvest all the trees in strips up to 200 feet (60 m) wide and 300 feet (90 m) long, or in square patches about 130 feet (40 m) on a side, to allow sunlight to reach the forest floor so new trees could grow (Thornton 1957; Benzie 1963; Johnston 1977). They left the forest between the strips or patches intact, with the idea that this would provide both seed for regeneration and winter cover for deer. Northern white-cedar did regenerate in

Strip cuts in a northern white-cedar stand in Maine.

some of the harvested strips and patches, but the seedlings often died before they reached the canopy (Miller et al. 1991; Heitzman et al. 1999). Although competition from faster-growing plants was part of the problem, most of the northern white-cedar seedlings were eaten by deer that sheltered in the adjacent intact forest (Verme and Johnston 1986; Van Deelen 1999). Apparently, deer tend to regard strips of small northern white-cedar trees as nature's equivalent of an all-you-can-eat buffet.

Silviculture guides now advise against trying to regenerate northern white-cedar where deer populations are high, unless steps can be taken to reduce browsing (Boulfroy et al. 2012). Though some protection may be provided by deep winter snow, management of deer or forest conditions is usually needed. In addition to reducing deer populations by hunting, physical barriers such as fences that prevent deer from reaching seedlings (exclosures) work well but can be costly. Scientists have suggested less expensive approaches to protecting seedlings, including leaving tree tops and branches in the forest after harvesting to create physical barriers (Verme and Johnston 1986; Smallidge and Chedzoy 2019), growing northern white-cedar seedlings in mixture with other species to distribute the effects of browsing (Herfindal et al. 2015), and clearing competing vegetation to help northern white-cedar saplings grow rapidly out of reach of deer (6 to 10 feet, 2 to 3 m) (Boulfroy et al. 2012). However, these recommendations are largely untested, and natural resource managers are reluctant to use approaches that might not produce desired results. So far, no one has found a reliable and cost-effective solution to regenerating northern white-cedar in areas where there are many deer.

Managing for Wood Production

Aside from efforts to maintain habitat for deer, early silvicultural efforts rarely focused on northern white-cedar. So, when natural resource managers became concerned about sustainability of northern white-cedar in the mid to late twentieth century, foresters had little guidance on how to proceed. To solve this problem, scientists worked to better understand the silvics (ecological characteristics) of northern white-cedar (see Appendix E) and identify the factors limiting the establishment and growth of seedlings. In particular, the transition from seedling to tree can be difficult for northern white-cedar. Scientists identified a number of limiting factors: insufficient seed due to past harvesting of mature northern white-cedar trees, unsuitable forest floor conditions for germination, slow seedling growth caused by competition from other species, and widespread mortality caused by excessive deer browsing (Cornett et al. 2000; Simard et al. 2003; Larouche and Ruel 2015). In light of this understanding, scientists advised slowly opening the canopy by harvesting trees gradually over time rather than all at once. They believed that this would provide a reliable seed source and give northern white-cedar seedlings time to establish and grow with little competition in the partial shade of their parent trees (Hannah 2004).

   With this knowledge, new approaches to northern white-cedar silviculture were developed. In stands where young, middle-aged, and old trees were growing together, scientists suggested periodically harvesting some trees— either individually or in small groups—to produce a steady supply of northern white-cedar products while maintaining trees of varying ages and partial shade on the forest floor (Van Deelen 1999; Boulfroy et al. 2012; Saucier et al. 2018). Silviculturists call this *selection cutting* or *irregular shelterwood cutting*. In northern white-cedar stands where the trees are all of similar age (for example, on abandoned pastureland in New England and Quebec), a different approach can

Harvesting operation to remove individual and small groups of northern white-cedar trees.

be used. If the trees are not yet mature, some of those that are growing poorly or are crowded can be harvested (Johnston 1972). This is called *thinning* and increases the resources available to the trees that remain, helping them grow faster. Once the trees are mature, they can be removed in two or more harvests over a number of years rather than all at once, so that new seedlings can start growing before the large trees providing seed and shade are removed (Hannah 2004). This is called *shelterwood cutting*.

Whether harvesting is intended to increase growth of remaining trees, create space for new seedlings, or both, it is important that loggers take care to protect highly decayed downed logs (nurse logs for seedlings), northern white-cedar seedlings already growing, and mature trees from machinery damage. This can be done by keeping machines on designated trails and controlling the direction of treefall during harvesting. This will help prevent damage that would allow fungi to enter northern white-cedar's fragile stems and shallow roots. Otherwise, stands that have been harvested may end up with many decayed stems (Hofmeyer et al. 2009).

Managing Uplands and Lowlands

Despite similarities in management objectives and approaches across habitat types, some aspects of northern white-cedar silviculture differ between upland and lowland communities. In uplands where northern white-cedar is a minor species, foresters might identify and manage pockets of northern white-cedar called *micro-stands* within larger stands composed of other species (Boulfroy et al. 2012; Lussier and Meek 2014). Also, because northern white-cedar seedlings are likely to die on uplands if the soil surface dries out or competition from other species is intense, loggers might consider scarifying (using machinery to scratch or mix) the surface of the forest floor on those sites during harvesting (Larouche et al. 2011). This exposes moisture-holding mineral soil for northern white-cedar seeds to germinate and kills competing plants already growing on the site. This would not be appropriate in lowlands where the water table is close to the soil surface or where northern white-cedar seedlings are already growing.

In pure or nearly pure stands of northern white-cedar, foresters can more easily prepare silviculture plans (prescriptions) to focus on this species than in stands where it grows in small quantities. Rather than managing small pockets of northern white-cedar, foresters managing old fields or lowlands where northern white-cedar is the dominant tree species can try to improve regeneration and

A micro-stand (patch) of northern white-cedar in a mixed-species conifer stand in Maine.

growth across entire stands. In lowlands where layering is common (see Sidebar 5), it is important to protect existing regeneration rather than rely solely on new seedlings from seed. In addition, it is critical that machines used for logging do not damage the small pits and mounds from fallen tree stems, stumps, and roots that serve as safe sites for regeneration during periods of high water. These can be protected by restricting harvesting to the winter when the ground is frozen and placing treetops and branches in machinery trails to protect the forest floor. Lowland northern white-cedar stands in which steps such as these have not been taken, or which have been degraded by road building or other types of construction, might need to be restored (see Sidebar 7).

Old Growth

Identifying stands where silviculture should not occur is an important part of managing forests and landscapes. Such stands might have high conservation value due to rare species, or represent a developmental stage that is uncommon

Pits and mounds in a lowland northern white-cedar stand.

on the landscape, like old growth. Old-growth northern white-cedar forests are extremely rare. Though exact acreage is unknown, scientists estimate that no more than 1% of the northern forest is old growth (Rusterholz 1996; Tester 1995; Davis 1996; Mosseler et al. 2003; Barton 2018). Within that, only a small fraction contains northern white-cedar. Because of its limited extent, old-growth northern white-cedar is at risk from threats such as nonnative invasive species and climate change.

Those of us who have been fortunate enough to visit old-growth forests know that they are magical places. Forests that have never been harvested and have had little to no human intervention for hundreds of years are very different from those that have been heavily disturbed by people. With the exception of some old-growth northern white-cedar on cliffs (Larson and Kelly 1991), most today are in swamps. These areas were never harvested because they are difficult to access or otherwise undesirable for logging. Here, the old, large trees have roughened bark, with soft patches of moss and branches draped with wisps of lichen called *old man's beard*. The j-shaped "pistol-butted" tree trunks curve up from the forest floor and lean in every direction, creating a labyrinth of stems to climb through.

Northern white-cedar tree growing on a stump that has rotted away, leaving it with stilt roots.

SIDEBAR 7 Northern White-Cedar Swamp Restoration

Rod A. Chimner

Northern white-cedar forests are valuable ecosystems because they store large amounts of carbon in their soils (Ott and Chimner 2016); provide valuable wildlife habitat; release cold, clean water to streams; and are one of the most biodiverse ecosystems throughout their range (Kost et al. 2007). Unfortunately, many northern white-cedar forests are in poor health, and it will require focused effort to restore them in both wetlands (swamps) and drier upland habitats (Palik et al. 2015; Kangas et al. 2016). Most of the work on restoring northern white-cedar on drier non-wetland areas entails using new forest management techniques, protecting young trees from being eaten by deer, hares, and other animals, and improving soil conditions so that a greater number of northern white-cedar seeds are able to sprout on the forest floor. These factors are also important for restoring northern white-cedar swamps. However, northern white-cedar swamps have other types of disturbances that require additional restoration techniques (Chimner et al. 2017).

Water is the most important factor in sustaining wetlands, and it is often the most important factor when restoring northern white-cedar swamps. Like all plants, northern white-cedar can tolerate a range of moisture conditions but will drown in too much water. Too little water is also problematic. Dead trees alongside many roads are a clear indication that northern white-cedar is susceptible to changes in the amount of water.

Roads built across wetlands often intercept groundwater. Groundwater is water that flows through soil rather than on its surface. Although groundwater is not usually visible, it is very important for most wetlands. Groundwater can pool against roadsides, causing floods that kill northern white-cedar, leave behind a stand of dead "ghost trees," and enable cattails to replace the forest.

Culverts are typically used to prevent flooding, as they allow the water to pass under the road. Although culverts can prevent flooded conditions, they also cause water to become and stay channelized, thus transforming slow-moving groundwater to fast-moving water. The resultant "stream channels" can erode soft wetland soil and effectively inhibit rewetting of the wetland soil on the other side of the road.

Northern white-cedar killed by inundation from a poorly designed road in Michigan.

Alteration of groundwater by roads can be widespread. In a field survey of the factors impacting 93 northern white-cedar swamps in three counties in northern Minnesota, forest managers identified roads as having the most frequent impact (through alteration of the amount of water), followed closely by deer browsing. As a consequence of this finding, my colleagues and I conducted experimental restoration projects on two permeable roadbed designs. This was done to test if roads can be modified to allow for a more natural flow of water under the road than occurs through a culvert. This unique type of roadbed was created by removing the existing roadbed and replacing it with several layers of rock and geotextile fabric: first a rock layer, then geotextile fabric, then a 12-inch (30-cm) layer of 4 to 6 inch (10 to 15 cm) diameter rock, and finally another layer of geotextile fabric. Culverts were also incorporated to enable more rapid transport of water across the road in the event of large flooding events.

Sequence of road restoration in a northern white-cedar swamp:
(a) roadbed was removed, geotextile was laid out, and rock was spread over the fabric;
(b) another layer of fabric and dirt were laid over the top of the rock;

(c) additional rock was placed at the toe of the slope over the fabric exposed below the gravel roadbed, and erosion blankets were placed over the disturbed surfaces alongside the road;

(d) finished road.

Initial results show that the roads appear to be functioning as designed. Rather than ponding behind the roads, water was flowing underneath, thereby maintaining natural water movement on both sides of the road as well as allowing the roads to be drivable during wet periods. Though promising, continual monitoring will be required to ensure that the new porous roadbed does not become blocked by sediment buildup or beaver activity, either of which could compromise the new road design and cause all the water to flow through the culverts.

The amount of water can also be modified by microtopography. While northern white-cedar swamps may look flat from a distance, the surface actually undulates with many small mounds (hummocks) and small water-filled depressions (pools) (Chimner and Hart 1996). This small-scale variation of the forest floor (microtopography) is an important tool for restoration. A project in northern Michigan incorporated building artificial microtopography to restore a northern white-cedar forested wetland on old farm fields (Kangas et al. 2016). Most forested wetlands are created on flat ground, often leveled with a bulldozer. In this project, however, my colleagues and I constructed artificial hummocks with a backhoe, planted them with northern white-cedar seedlings, and compared the results with northern white-cedar we planted on flat ground. After five years, we found that seedlings planted on hummocks had a 75% survival rate compared to only a 15% survival rate when planted on flat areas. In addition, northern white-cedar seedlings grew much faster on the hummocks (12 inches or 30 cm per year) compared to flat areas (3 inches or 8 cm per year) (Kangas et al. 2016).

In the Great Lakes region, most northern white-cedar swamps that have been logged have not returned to northern white-cedar as might have been expected. Instead, they have been replaced by species such as tag alder, balsam fir, and red maple (Chimner and Hart 1996; Heitzman et al. 1997). A study by the Michigan Department of Natural Resources showed that even fifty years after an experimental cutting in a northern white-cedar swamp near Marquette, Michigan, northern white-cedar regeneration was still absent, with tag alder and balsam fir dominating the cut areas.

Since natural regeneration of northern white-cedar is often low in northern white-cedar swamps after forest harvests, my colleagues and I examined the effectiveness of hand-planting northern white-cedar seedlings as an option for restoring northern white-cedar in swamps. Thousands of northern white-cedar seedlings were hand-planted in five former northern white-cedar swamps in northern Minnesota. Because deer and other animals are known to eat most young northern white-cedar seedlings, the study also tested whether using small fences to enclose individual seedlings improved survival. For two years after planting, we monitored survival and growth, along with other potentially important factors such as microtopography, deer browsing, and amount of light that reached the seedlings. Initial results showed that roughly half of all planted seedlings survived, with microtopography having the greatest impact. Northern white-cedar had poor survival if they were planted in wet depressions (about 20%) and much better survival if they were planted on higher and drier hummocks (about 60%). The northern white-cedar trees also grew much faster when planted on hummocks. The small single-tree fencing also helped protect the young northern white-cedar from being eaten by deer.

Northern white-cedar swamps are an important ecosystem but have undergone many detrimental changes through the years. Understanding the natural flow and amount of water is of the utmost importance when trying to restore northern white-cedar swamps. Reestablishing the natural flow of water is often a vital first step in the restoration of northern white-cedar swamps; however, many other types of restoration activities are often needed to fully achieve the desired outcome of a healthy ecosystem.

Northern white-cedar trees with spiral grain—a twisted growth pattern thought to be a genetic adaptation to wind (Skatter and Kucera 1998)—are common. Many of the trees have broken tops and dead branches from years of wind and ice exposure. Downed logs are strewn about and range from freshly fallen stems to those indistinguishable from the moss-covered forest floor. Shafts of sunlight appear in openings created by fallen trees, illuminating seedlings and layers that have been waiting beneath the canopy for their chance to race to the sky.

And yet scientists have long struggled to define old growth. They generally agree that old-growth forests have high proportions of canopy trees near their maximum life span and have had little to no human disturbance. In simple terms, these forests are relatively old and undisturbed by people (Hunter

Old-growth northern white-cedar in Big Reed Forest Reserve, Maine. *(Photo by Nathan Wesely)*

1989). Even using those loose criteria, it can be difficult to tell if a northern white-cedar stand is old growth. Because they often grow slowly and can live a long time, northern white-cedar trees may be hundreds of years old and quite small, even if growing in forests where logging occurred. And it can be difficult to determine the ages of these trees because so many are hollow. Scientists have suggested that attributes other than tree age could be used, such as presence of rare lichens (Selva 2003).

In addition to preserving these forests, there is interest in increasing old-growth characteristics in managed forests. Scientists working in Maine and New Brunswick have observed that old-growth northern white-cedar forests in swamps and seeps in that region have low rates of canopy disturbance, many highly decayed fallen logs, and large average tree size (Wesely et al. 2018; Fraver et al. 2020). Some of those features—small canopy gaps, fallen logs, and large trees—can be maintained in harvested stands. Silviculture of this type is called *ecological forestry*. While harvested northern white-cedar stands with these characteristics do not provide all the values of old-growth forest, they do

Northern white-cedar tree with spiral grain. *(Photo by Nathan Wesely)*

provide some of the structures important to plants and animals found in stands with mature trees and low rates of canopy disturbance (Bauhus et al. 2009).

Scaling Up

Scientists have long debated whether management should focus on a few key species or many species, but generally agree that conflicts and tradeoffs are unavoidable. Northern white-cedar is no exception. Management aimed at maintaining large numbers of deer in the northern forest has not proven compatible with management for northern white-cedar. This has implications for many other plants and animals that live in those communities. In addition, though silviculture decisions are usually made at the scale of stands or harvest units, a landscape-level approach is needed to balance competing values at a larger scale. Regardless of the decisions individual landowners make, long-term planning for both preservation and active management of northern white-cedar is important. Harvesting moratoria have been enacted on some publicly owned lands but are short-term solutions to habitat management problems. Yet, the long-term sustainability of northern white-cedar communities—and the human communities that harvest, process, and use the wood—requires thoughtful approaches to balancing competing concerns. Though the outcomes people desire and the approaches they prefer vary, sustainability of the northern white-cedar resource depends on not just short-term results but long-term outcomes. Viewed through the lens of uncertainty that comes with climate change, efforts to improve the vigor of northern white-cedar trees and ensure that the forest includes healthy trees of all ages and sizes is important to ensure resilience in the future.

CHAPTER 8

Conservation of Northern White-Cedar: What We Can Do Now

Despite promising avenues for management, it is easy to feel discouraged by the condition of northern white-cedar in much of its range today. Since European settlement, our actions have directly or indirectly decreased the abundance of this species in the northern forest region as a whole. Even where northern white-cedar is abundant, the condition of the trees and its natural communities is too often degraded. Repeated, preferential harvesting of the biggest and least-decayed trees, frequent disturbances that create opportunities for competing and nonnative invasive plants to grow, and construction projects that disrupt water movement have impacted northern white-cedar to its detriment (see Sidebar 7).

To some degree, this pattern mirrors that of other species in the region. Yet while it is true that there are many fewer acres of forestland than before Europeans arrived, individual tree species have responded in different ways. Those that produce large amounts of seed, sprout readily, and grow rapidly—such as red maple and aspen—have become prolific in forests from which we have

Degraded northern white-cedar stand with an understory of shrubs.

heavily and repeatedly harvested trees. Tree species like northern white-cedar have been less successful in recent centuries, in part because they have a conservative growth strategy. This served them well in forests with little human disturbance, enabling them to survive in low light beneath the crowns of larger trees, slowly ascend into the canopy, and eventually become dominant by outlasting their faster-growing, shorter-lived neighbors. Species like these also tend to produce relatively fewer seeds and have fragile seedlings that survive better on moist, decayed logs than in dead leaves (leaf litter) on the forest floor. But harvesting often increases the amount of light reaching the forest floor, sometimes diminishes the amount of seed by removing mature trees, and always reduces the number of decayed logs by removing trees from the forest before they die and fall down. As if that were not enough to overcome, northern white-cedar has the added disadvantage of being a preferred food for a number of species, most notably the white-tailed deer that we seek to maintain at high densities in parts of its range.

In addition to considering the present condition of northern white-cedar, we need to make plans for the future. If we restrict our discussion of management to silviculture involving harvesting (the prevalent approach to actively managing trees), then it is clear that our capacity and willingness to manage northern white-cedar have diminished. Northern white-cedar forests on many public lands are subject to harvesting moratoria, even where the trees are abundant, because managers are unable to reliably regenerate new trees. We are fortunate that northern white-cedar trees are exceptionally long-lived among northern forest species—frequently reaching hundreds of years of age—because we have had the luxury of not addressing the problem. But all trees eventually die. And though dead northern white-cedar trees provide numerous benefits—including as nurse logs or mounds for regeneration of their own offspring from seed—new trees will be needed to grow and ascend into the canopy. So far, foresters have not found reliable and cost-effective ways to grow small northern white-cedar where deer densities are high. The debate over appropriate deer densities and the social and economic implications of managing deer herds suggest that an easy solution is not near at hand.

We would also be wise to consider whether northern white-cedar and its communities can adapt to recent and predicted environmental changes. Given that this species has been growing in northern forests since the glaciers retreated thousands of years ago, the last few hundred years are mere moments in its long history. Yet we know from scientists' observations and predictions of climate

Natural mortality of northern white-cedar trees from blowdown in Maine.

change that more changes are on the way, at a rate much faster than those of similar magnitude in the past. As this change occurs, natural communities as we know them will transform in small and large ways that reflect individual species' abilities to relocate or adapt to new conditions. Given the compressed time scale, it is reasonable to conclude that our assistance will be needed in creating a sustainable future for today's natural communities. Within this context, our capacity to achieve the future we want for northern white-cedar depends on our attention to a number of key values we tried to convey in the pages of this book.

Ecological Values

It doesn't seem adequate to say that northern white-cedar is ecologically important, because anyone familiar with the interconnectedness of the natural world would be unlikely to say that any species is unimportant. Nevertheless, there is convincing evidence that the presence of northern white-cedar has far-reaching implications for its communities. From forested wetlands to rocky summits, northern white-cedar provides a seemingly endless list of benefits to everything from tiny miners in its leaves to black bears clawing at its stems. Rare plants, lichens, and fungi abound with many sensitive sites and unique dependencies. Who knows what else, like the myriad fungi working their magic beneath the forest floor, has been hidden from our view? There is no doubt that there are many more relationships that have yet to be discovered. In all our dealings with northern white-cedar, as with all natural communities, we must hold these ecological values paramount.

Social Values

Northern white-cedar has been an integral part of human existence for thousands of years. Indigenous peoples have had spiritual and utilitarian relationships with this species since long before Europeans ever set foot in the northern forest. After Europeans arrived, people increasingly turned to agriculture and industry for their livelihoods, physically and psychologically distancing themselves from the natural world. As a result, we lost many of the connections our ancestors had to the native plants and animals that sustain us. Few people outside of Indigenous cultures today have a spiritual connection to trees. Too often we seek the products of trees—shingles for our homes, posts for our fences, or mulch for our gardens—without considering whether we are using

Northern white-cedar trees in Gooseberry Falls State Park, Minnesota; these trees were called *soulmates* by the photographer. *(Photo by Susanne von Schroeder)*

the resource sustainably. Even worse, we use these products while calling for preservation of forests we enjoy, passing exploitation off to locations for which we have less affection (scientists call this *leakage*: efforts to protect one area merely displace losses to another). In order to sustain the values of northern white-cedar—employment for people working in the northern forest, recreation and hunting opportunities, wood products, and the many other values it provides—we must educate ourselves about its natural communities and advocate for responsible use.

Variability

Though northern white-cedar remains one of the most common tree species in parts of its range, it has been greatly diminished in others. High variability in the condition of northern white-cedar trees and forests across its range means that different approaches to conservation are warranted in different places. Where large populations of this tree species intersect with small populations of deer, there are many opportunities for management with a high probability

Abundant northern white-cedar saplings in northern Maine where white-tailed deer densities are low. *(Photo by Andrew P. Richley)*

of success if silviculture guidance is followed. However, there are other places, particularly in the Lake States, where northern white-cedar regeneration is very difficult to secure regardless of the amount of this species in the canopy (see Appendix C). In order to sustain northern white-cedar and its many values, we must find ways to manage it in those places too, not just where it is easy to do so. Coordinating northern white-cedar management with deer management seems like a necessary first step, but one that will be difficult to take until more voices participate in the conversation.

Moving Forward

Those engaged in natural resource management often distinguish between preservation and conservation. Preservation is protecting natural communities by designating them off-limits to human intervention to the greatest degree possible, while conservation is protecting natural communities while using them sustainably. This distinction is not trivial. While preservation is an important tool in forest management, it does not allow us to extract wood or wildlife. As long as people continue to work and live in rural northern forest communities—and as long as we continue to not only prefer but increasingly rely upon renewable natural resources—preservation alone cannot meet our needs.

With this in mind, a thoughtful approach to sustaining northern white-cedar requires that we pursue many avenues at the same time. First, we must identify additional areas for preservation and work to maintain the integrity of those already preserved. These might be on sensitive sites, contain old growth, or provide homes for rare, threatened, or endangered plants and animals. Natural communities that are uncommon in the places where they are found (even if common elsewhere) are also good candidates for preservation, as are those that are exemplary, unspoiled examples of their type. In addition, places that are not particularly special by any objective measure might not be suitable for management for reasons unique to the landowner. Many degraded woodlots are loved by the people who own them and need not be actively managed if that is not the owners' desire. In the context of millions of acres with northern white-cedar trees, preserving lands in all these categories still leaves the majority for other types of management.

Second, we must continue to engage in active management of northern white-cedar where the trees are abundant. This can take many forms, focused on producing wood, creating wildlife habitat or old-growth characteristics, or all of

Northern white-cedar at Jordan Pond overlooking the Bubbles in Acadia National Park, Maine.

Northern white-cedar tree with cavities excavated by a woodpecker.

A stump from a harvested northern white-cedar tree with decay, smiling.

these and more. On sites degraded by road construction, mining, development, or past mismanagement, restoration activities may be warranted (see Sidebar 7). Planting (and protecting, if necessary) even a few northern white-cedar trees is a way each of us can contribute to the sustainability of this species and the many values it provides. Regardless of our motivation for management or the approach we use, any attempt to regenerate northern white-cedar is unlikely to succeed where deer densities are high. In those areas, the best solution is to reduce deer populations through action and advocacy. Any other approaches—fencing to exclude deer, using slash to limit their movement, or reducing competition around small trees to help them grow more quickly—are temporary, often expensive, and unreliable fixes to a widespread and persistent problem.

Thinking more broadly, taking steps to combat climate change is perhaps the single most important thing we can do not only for northern white-cedar but all natural communities. Reducing greenhouse gas emissions, increasing the amount of carbon stored in forests and wood products, and increasing the rate of carbon uptake in growing trees are all necessary to slow climate change.

As we tackle this whole-earth endeavor, we can also engage in management to improve and maintain the health and vigor of forests and trees, including northern white-cedar. Being a climate change "loser" (Iverson et al. 2008) doesn't mean we should give up on this species. Forests with different ages of healthy trees, with adequate access to water and light, and free from insect pests and diseases are more likely to be resilient to environmental stressors in the future.

As we face the uncertainty of the future, take solace in what we have now. Notice the cedar chest in your home, the mulch in your garden, the tree in the park, and think about the tiny miners in the leaves, the squirrels shredding the bark, the black bear cubs climbing the trunks, and all the ways this tree and others link us together with the rest of the natural world. It is our hope that what you have learned in this book about northern white-cedar—an unassuming, medium-sized, seemingly unremarkable tree—has inspired you to look more carefully, think more deeply, and speak more loudly about not only charismatic species but also the many and intricate connections in natural communities. These will not be easy tasks, and there will be adversity and failure. As you face these, the best advice we can give you is this: be more like northern white-cedar: patient, persistent, resourceful, and resilient. And if you fall and find yourself in an unfamiliar place, put down roots and start again.

Common and Scientific
Names of Plants

JEANETTE ALLOGIO

Trees

Alaska-cedar	*Callitropsis nootkatensis*
American basswood	*Tilia americana*
American elm	*Ulmus americana*
Ash	*Fraxinus* spp.
Aspen	*Populus* spp.
Atlantic white-cedar	*Chamaecyparis thyoides*
Balsam fir	*Abies balsamea*
Birch	*Betula* spp.
Black ash	*Fraxinus nigra*
Black spruce	*Picea mariana*
Canada yew	*Taxus canadensis*
Cedar	*Cedrus* spp.
Cedar of Lebanon	*Cedrus libani*
Cherry	*Prunus* spp.
Eastern hemlock	*Tsuga canadensis*
Eastern redcedar	*Juniperus virginiana*
Eastern white pine	*Pinus strobus*
Glossy buckthorn	*Frangula alnus*

Juniper	*Juniperus* spp.
Mountain-ash	*Sorbus* spp.
Mountain paper birch	*Betula papyrifera* var. *cordifolia*
Northern white-cedar; Arborvitae	*Thuja occidentalis*
Oriental-arborvitae	*Platycladus orientalis*
Paper birch; White birch	*Betula papyrifera*
Pin cherry	*Prunus pensylvanica*
Pine	*Pinus* spp.
Quaking aspen	*Populus tremuloides*
Red maple	*Acer rubrum*
Red pine	*Pinus resinosa*
Red spruce	*Picea rubens*
Redwood	*Sequoia sempervirens*
Spruce	*Picea* spp.
Sugar maple	*Acer saccharum*
Tamarack	*Larix laricina*
Western redcedar	*Thuja plicata*
White ash	*Fraxinus americana*
White spruce	*Picea glauca*
Yellow birch	*Betula alleghaniensis*

Shrubs

Alder	*Alnus* spp.
American fly honeysuckle	*Lonicera canadensis*
Beaked hazel	*Corylus cornuta*
Blueberry	*Vaccinium* spp.
Common juniper	*Juniperus communis*
Creeping juniper	*Juniperus horizontalis*
Dogwood	*Cornus* spp.
Dwarf red blackberry	*Rubus pubescens*
Elderberry	*Sambucus* spp.
Holly	*Ilex* spp.
Honeysuckle	*Lonicera* spp.
Lapland rosebay	*Rhododendron lapponicum*
Lowbush blueberry	*Vaccinium angustifolium*
Mountain maple	*Acer spicatum*

Northern mountain cranberry	*Vaccinium vitis-idaea* ssp. *minus*
Raspberry	*Rubus* spp.
Red elderberry	*Sambucus racemosa*
Speckled alder	*Alnus incana*
Sumac	*Rhus* spp.
Tag alder	*Alnus serrulata*
Wild sarsaparilla	*Aralia nudicaulis*
Willow	*Salix* spp.

Herbaceous Plants, Grasses, Sedges, Ferns, and Mosses

American ginseng	*Panax quinquefolius*
Bluebell bellflower	*Campanula rotundifolia*
Cattail	*Typha* spp.
Cinnamon fern	*Osmunda cinnamomea*
Common butterwort	*Pinguicula vulgaris*
Dicranum moss	*Dicranum* spp.
Dwarf lake iris	*Iris lacustris*
Fairy slipper	*Calypso bulbosa*
False Solomon's seal	*Maianthemum racemosum*
Giant rattlesnake-plantain	*Goodyera oblongifolia*
Hairy Solomon's seal	*Polygonatum pubescens*
Heartleaf foamflower	*Tiarella cordifolia*
Indian-cucumber	*Medeola virginiana*
Long beech fern	*Phegopteris connectilis*
Marsh thistle	*Cirsium palustre*
Mountain woodsorrel	*Oxalis montana*
Northern blue monkshood	*Aconitum noveboracense*
Orange jewelweed	*Impatiens capensis*
Phragmites, common reed	*Phragmites australis*
Purple loosestrife	*Lythrum salicaria*
Ram's head lady's slipper	*Cypripedium arietinum*
Red columbine	*Aquilegia canadensis*
Reed canarygrass	*Phalaris arundinacea*
Roundleaf orchid	*Amerorchis rotundifolia*
Shining clubmoss	*Huperzia lucidula*
Showy lady's slipper	*Cypripedium reginae*

Starflower	*Trientalis borealis*
Sphagnum moss	*Sphagnum* spp.
Threeleaf goldthread	*Coptis trifolia*
Wildrice	*Zizania* spp.
Woodfern	*Dryopteris* spp.
Yellow jewelweed	*Impatiens pallida*

Source: U.S. Department of Agriculture, Natural Resources Conservation Service (2021).

Common and Scientific Names of Animals

Birds

American tree sparrow	*Spizella arborea*
Black-backed woodpecker	*Picoides arcticus*
Common redpoll	*Acanthis flammea*
Pileated woodpecker	*Dryocopus pileatus*
Pine siskin	*Carduelis pinus*
Ruffed grouse	*Bonasa umbellus*
Slate-colored junco	*Junco hyemalis*
Spruce grouse	*Canachites canadensis*
Three-toed woodpecker	*Picoides dorsalis*
Warbler	*Dendroica* spp.

Mammals

Beaver	*Castor canadensis*
Black bear	*Ursus americanus*
Bobcat	*Lynx rufus*
Coyote	*Canis latrans*
Elk	*Cervus elaphus*

Gray wolf	*Canis lupus*
Least chipmunk	*Eutamias minimus*
Moose	*Alces alces*
Northern flying squirrel	*Glaucomys volans*
Porcupine	*Erethizon dorsatum*
Red squirrel	*Tamiasciurus hudsonicus*
Snowshoe hare	*Lepus americanus*
White-tailed deer	*Odocoileus virginianus*

Insects and Snails

Arborvitae leafminer	*Argyresthia thuiella*
Japanese cedar longhorn beetle	*Callidiellum rufipenne*
Carpenter ant	*Camponotus* spp.
Cherrystone drop land snail	*Hendersonia occulta*

The Northern White-Cedar Resource in the United States

CHRISTOPHER W. WOODALL

As is the case with any tree species in the United States, the course of northern white-cedar existence over the past few hundred years has generally followed dynamics common to forests more broadly. Individual tree species were greatly affected as the United States expanded westward from colonies highly dependent on forest resources and deforestation activities (i.e., agricultural and urban/industrial development) to our contemporary period. Today, forestland has largely stabilized in the United States, but with a suite of potentially negative global change factors impacting forests, such as browsing, insects and disease, climate change, invasive plants, and fragmentation. Northern white-cedar is in many ways unique, but when trends in forest resources are examined, we can see that it is not that much different from other tree species. It is a dynamic species within a context of an ever-changing landscape.

The data used to make the graphs below were collected by the U.S. Forest Service, Forest Inventory and Analysis program, using annual inventories of forests across the nation. Assessments such as these help natural resource managers and policymakers interpret the status of species of interest, and of forests as a whole. This summary does not include Canada, but provides a useful perspective of the northern white-cedar resource in the United States.

Change among Species and Trends in Number of Trees

The following infographic shows rank, total estimate, and percent change of northern white-cedar abundance compared to other tree species in eastern U.S. forests over the past two decades. This includes number of living and dead northern white-cedar trees in various size classes and amount of carbon stored in those trees. The tree sizes of interest to foresters are used in this summary. These are based on diameter of the stem at chest height (called *diameter at breast height* or *dbh*) and include seedlings (smaller than 1 inch or 2.5 cm), saplings (1 to 4.9 inches; 2.5 to 7.6 cm), poletimber (5.0 to 9.9 inches; 7.7 to 25.4 cm), and sawtimber (10 inches or 25.5 cm and larger) (Figure 1). Out of 341 tree species, northern white-cedar has been ranked between 15th and 30th in terms of number of standing dead and live trees in most size classes over the

FIGURE 1. Past (Time 1: 1998–2011) and current (Time 2: 2012–2019) rank, total estimate, and percent change of northern white-cedar compared to all other tree species for various resource metrics (all estimates are number of trees while carbon is tons) in eastern U.S. forests.

past two decades. The number of northern white-cedar trees has increased in all size classes except seedlings, with a notable increase in the number of large (sawtimber-size) trees. Tons of carbon stored in northern white-cedar trees increased during this time.

Proportions of Trees

Another aspect of tree populations that is useful for understanding sustainability is abundance of northern white-cedar seedlings and saplings in stands with varying amounts of northern white-cedar in the overstory (Figure 2). This helps natural resource managers determine if there are imbalances, such as too few small trees, and if so, where they need to focus management efforts. These data show that as the proportion of northern white-cedar in the overstory

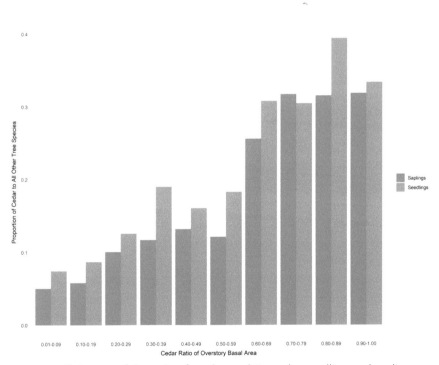

FIGURE 2. Estimates of the ratio of northern white-cedar seedling and sapling abundance compared to all competing tree species by classes of northern white-cedar live tree basal area (the cross-sectional area of tree stems) for trees 5 inches (12.7 cm) dbh and larger for coterminous U.S. forests, 2012–2019.

increases, so too does the proportion of this species in the understory. Yet, even where northern white-cedar is the most abundant species in the overstory, it rarely accounts for more than 3 out of 10 seedlings or saplings. In fact, there is little change in the proportion of northern white-cedar in the understory as overstory proportion increases from 0.6 to a pure cedar composition. In addition, the ratio of northern white-cedar saplings to other tree species is generally lower than the ratio of northern white-cedar seedlings to other tree species. This suggests that relatively fewer northern white-cedar seedlings are reaching sapling size compared to those of other tree species.

Hotspots of Resource Change

Identifying areas where there are large changes in forest attributes such as amount of growth, harvest, or mortality is important for evaluating sustainability of stands of different ages, compositions, or structures. The images below are heat maps that show amount of change in different states for northern white-cedar (Figure 3).

These heat maps show that the amplitude and direction of population changes differ across the region. Maine, for example, is a hotspot for increasing numbers of northern white-cedar seedlings, while the Upper Peninsula of Michigan has hotspots for increasing numbers of saplings, poles, and sawtimber. Yet there are also hotspots of sapling or poletimber loss in the Upper Peninsula and northern Wisconsin. In addition, these areas are hotspots of increasing standing deadwood abundance resulting from mortality of northern white-cedar trees. Collectively, the gross gains and losses for aspects of the cedar resource underlie the net trajectory of these forest resources into the future.

Taken together, these summaries show that though the northern white-cedar resource is dynamic, the challenges that natural resource managers face when managing this species are not the same in all regions or all stand types. Nevertheless, a general trend of relatively fewer trees of smaller sizes and increases in the number of larger, likely older trees supports the need to think strategically about managing the northern white-cedar resource.

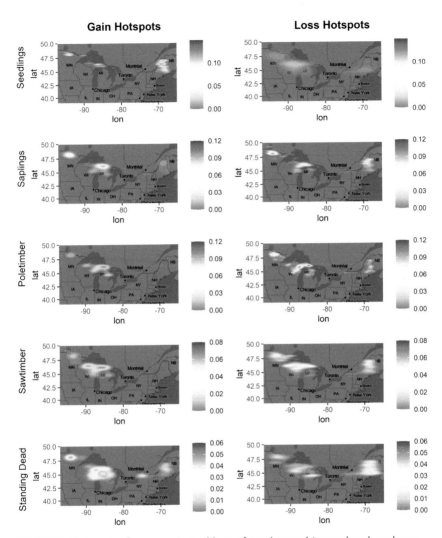

FIGURE 3. Hotspots of gross gain and loss of northern white-cedar abundance for seedlings through standing dead trees, 2012–2019. Axes are latitude and longitude. Legend scale is the interpolated density of inventory observations with higher densities indicating a greater spatial occurrence of observations.

Rare Plants in Northern White-Cedar Communities

The following are common and scientific names (USDA Natural Resources Conservation Service 2021) and status of rare plants associated with selected swamp natural community types dominated by northern white-cedar in Michigan, Wisconsin, and Maine. Species that are state-listed as Special Concern, Threatened, or Endangered are included.

Michigan

RICH CONIFER SWAMP
   Associated Rare Plants in Type

Common Name	Scientific Name	State Legal Status
Black crowberry	*Empetrum nigrum*	Threatened
Common butterwort	*Pinguicula vulgaris*	Special Concern
Fairy slipper	*Calypso bulbosa*	Threatened
Fleshy starwort	*Stellaria crassifolia*	Threatened
Giant mountain aster	*Canadanthus modestus*	Threatened
Houghton's goldenrod	*Solidago houghtonii*	Threatened
Hudson Bay sedge	*Carex heleonastes*	Endangered

Common Name	Scientific Name	State Legal Status
Hyssopleaf fleabane	*Erigeron hyssopifolius*	Threatened
Lapland buttercup	*Ranunculus lapponicus*	Threatened
Marsh grass-of-Parnassus	*Parnassia palustris*	Threatened
Michigan monkeyflower	*Mimulus glabratus* var. *michiganensis*	Endangered
Northern mountain cranberry	*Vaccinium vitis-idaea* ssp. *minus*	Endangered
Ram's head lady's slipper	*Cypripedium arietinum*	Special Concern
Roundleaf orchid	*Amerorchis rotundifolia*	Endangered
Scented oakfern	*Gymnocarpium robertianum*	Threatened
Twinberry honeysuckle	*Lonicera involucrata*	Threatened

Source: Kost et al. 2007; Michigan State University n.d.

Wisconsin

NORTHERN WET-MESIC FOREST (WHITE-CEDAR SWAMP)
Associated Rare Plants in Type

Common Name	Scientific Name	State Legal Status
Fairy slipper	*Calypso bulbosa*	Threatened
Lapland buttercup	*Ranunculus lapponicus*	Endangered
Marsh valerian	*Valeriana uliginosa*	Threatened
Northern mountain cranberry	*Vaccinium vitis-idaea* ssp. *minus*	Endangered
Ram's head lady's slipper	*Cypripedium arietinum*	Threatened
Roundleaf orchid	*Amerorchis rotundifolia*	Threatened
Scented oakfern	*Gymnocarpium robertianum*	Special Concern
Western Jacob's-ladder	*Polemonium occidentale* ssp. *lacustre*	Endangered

Sources: Epstein et al. 2002; Wisconsin Department of Natural Resources n.d.

Maine

NORTHERN WHITE-CEDAR SWAMP

Associated Rare Plants in Type

Common Name	Scientific Name	State Legal Status
Lapland buttercup	Ranunculus lapponicus	Threatened
Livid sedge	Carex livida	Special Concern
Northern bog bedstraw	Galium labradoricum	Special Concern
Northern bog sedge	Carex gynocrates	Special Concern
Roundleaf orchid	Amerorchis rotundifolia	Threatened
Sageleaf willow	Salix candida	Endangered
Showy lady's slipper	Cypripedium reginae	Special Concern
Sparseflower sedge	Carex tenuiflora	Special Concern
White adder's-mouth orchid	Malaxis brachypoda	Endangered

Sources: Gawler and Cutko 2010; Maine Department of Agriculture, Conservation and Forestry 2015.

Silvical Characteristics
of Northern White-Cedar

Commonly Associated Tree Species

Balsam fir (*Abies balsamea*), black ash (*Fraxinus nigra*), black spruce (*Picea mariana*), eastern hemlock (*Tsuga canadensis*), eastern white pine (*Pinus strobus*), paper birch (*Betula papyrifera*), quaking aspen (*Populus tremuloides*), red maple (*Acer rubrum*), tamarack (*Larix laricina*), white spruce (*Picea glauca*), and yellow birch (*Betula allegheniensis*).

Soil Preference

Best growth occurs on neutral or alkaline mineral soils of limestone origin (i.e., high in calcium). In swamps, site quality for northern white-cedar increases as drainage improves and peat depth decreases. Composition of the organic material is important; peat comprised of moderately to well-decomposed woody plants or sedges is reportedly preferred by northern white-cedar. Source: Wisconsin Department of Natural Resources (2019).

Silvical Characteristics

Pollination	Male pollen cones and female seed cones form on branchlets of the same tree. Pollination is by wind from late April to the early part of June.

Cones	Mature cone formation begins by mid- to late June. Cone growth is complete by mid-August with cone opening beginning late summer. The interval between cone ripening and cone opening is short, about 7 to 10 days.
Seed dispersal	Most seed are dispersed by November, but some seed falls throughout the winter. Seed is wind-dispersed, but because northern white-cedar trees are usually not very tall, the effective seeding range is 150 to 200 feet (45 to 60 m) except during unusually high winds.
Good seed years	Good seed crops occur every 2 to 5 years, with light to medium crops intervening. Seed production has been reported at less than 10 years, but adequate seed production usually starts at 30 years of age and is best after 75 years of age.
Germination	Normally begins in May or June in the year following seed dispersal. Seedlings often develop on decayed wood or organic matter, peat, or sphagnum moss (all of which provide warm microsites and access to moisture), but northern white-cedar does very well on seedbeds of exposed mineral soil (including trails and landings where the soil surface has been scarified by logging operations). Partial sunlight produces the best germination and seedling establishment rates.
Seed viability	Seed shows only slight internal dormancy. Germinative capacity is only about 35% under test conditions (Schopmeyer 1974).
Seedling development	Seedlings require constant water supply and establish well under partial canopy cover. Height growth of seedlings beneath the canopy is slow but increases with increasing light (Larouche et al. 2011). Elevated microsites (mounds, decayed logs

or stumps) are important for seedling survival on lowland sites with seasonally high water table.

Growth	Northern white-cedar generally grows more slowly than associated species, and is longer lived, reaching ages of 400 years or more on some sites (and rarely 1,000 years or more on the Niagara Escarpment; Larson and Kelly 1991). It is medium sized, commonly 40 to 50 feet (12 to 15 m), though rarely 80 feet (25 m) or taller. Diameter can be 2 to 3 feet (0.6 to 0.9 m). On average sites it takes 80 to 100 years to grow to pole size (about 5 inches or 12.7 cm in diameter at chest height); trees in the open and especially in plantations can grow much faster. Seedlings and layers often grow slowly beneath an overstory of larger trees and ascend to the canopy following multiple periods of suppression and release (Ruel et al. 2014; Fraver et al. 2020).
Shade tolerance	Northern white-cedar is shade tolerant and able to withstand suppression for many years. It responds well to release even at advanced ages.
Vegetative reproduction	Layering is a common means of northern white-cedar regeneration, particularly on lowland sites (swamps and seeps). Layers can originate from fallen trees, branches of standing trees, or seedlings and saplings (see Sidebar 5).
Major pests	Fungi—white stringy butt rot (*Perenniporia subacida*), balsam butt rot (*Polyporus balsameus*), and brown cubical rot (*Phaelous schweinitzii*)—can affect this tree. Serious insect pests are few, but Arborvitae leafminer (*Argyresthia thuiella*) can cause growth reduction and mortality.
Other considerations	Because northern white-cedar is a relatively shallow-rooted tree, it is subject to windthrow and uprooting.

Flooding, high water table, and slow-moving or stagnant groundwater can reduce growth rates and kill trees or stands. Mortality from hydrologic disruptions caused by beaver activity and road construction is common.

Northern white-cedar is a preferred winter browse for white-tailed deer and snowshoe hare, both in terms of palatability and nutrition. Browsing can be extensive, slow tree growth, and kill smaller trees, causing recruitment failures. Hare damage is sometimes as great as deer damage.

Sources: Fowells 1965; Johnston 1990; Boulfroy et al. 2012, except where noted.

BIBLIOGRAPHY

Aaseng, N. E., J. C. Almendinger, R. P. Dana, B. C. Delaney, H. L. Dunevitz, K. A. Rusterholz, N. P. Sather, and D. S. Wovcha. 1993. "Minnesota's Native Vegetation: A Key to Natural Communities, Version 1.5." (Minnesota Department of Natural Resources, Natural Heritage Program, Biological Report 20).

Aldous, S. E. 1941. "Deer Management Suggestions for Northern White Cedar Types." *Journal of Wildlife Management* 5: 90–94.

Alverson, W. S., D. M. Waller, and S. L. Solheim. 1988. "Forests Too Deer: Edge Effects in Northern Wisconsin." *Conservation Biology* 2: 348–358.

Anwar, G., E. A. Lilleskov, and R. A. Chimner. 2020. "Arbuscular Mycorrhizal Inoculation Has Similar Benefits to Fertilization for *Thuja occidentalis* L. Seedling Nutrition and Growth on Peat Soil over a Range of Ph: Implications for Restoration." *New Forests* 51: 297–311.

Bai, L., W. Wang, J. Hua, Z. Guo, and S. Luo. 2020. "Defensive Functions of Volatile Organic Compounds and Essential Oils from Northern White-Cedar in China." *BMC Plant Biology* 20, no. 1: 500.

Barton, A. M. 2018. "Introduction: Ecological and Historical Context." In *Ecology and Recovery of Eastern Old-Growth Forests*, edited by A. M. Barton and W. S. Keeton, 1–20. Washington, DC: Island Press.

Bauhus, J., K. Puettmann, and C. Messier. 2009. "Silviculture for Old-Growth Attributes." *Forest Ecology and Management* 258: 525–537.

Bazinet, N. L., and M. K. Sears. 1979. "Factors Affecting the Mortality of Leafminers *Argyresthia thuiella* and *Pulicalvaria thujaella* (Lepidoptera: Yponomeutidae and Gelechiidae) on Eastern White Cedar in Ontario." *Canadian Entomologist* 111, no. 11: 1299–1306.

Beaudoin, A., P. Y. Bernier, P. Villemaire, L. Guindon, and X. J. Guo. 2017. "Species Composition, Forest Properties and Land Cover Types across Canada's Forests at 250m Resolution for 2001 and 2011." Quebec: Natural Resources Canada, Canadian Forest Service, Laurentian Forestry Centre. https://doi.org/10.23687/ec9e2659-1c29-4ddb-87a2-6aced147a990.

Benzie, J. W. 1963. "Cutting Methods in Mixed Conifer Swamps, Upper Michigan." (U.S. Forest Service Research Paper LS-4). St. Paul, MN: U.S. Department of Agriculture, Forest Service, Lake States Forest Experiment Station.

Botti, W. 1991. "Condition of the Northern White-Cedar Resource." In *1990 Workshop Proceedings for the Northern White-Cedar in Michigan* (Res. Rep. 512), edited by D. O. Lantagne, 44–46. East Lansing: Michigan State University, Michigan Agricultural Experiment Station.

Boulanger, J. R., P. D. Curtis, E. V. Cooch, and A. J. DeNicola. 2012. "Sterilization as an Alternative Deer Control Technique: A Review." *Human–Wildlife Interactions* 6, no. 2: 273–282.

Boulfroy, E., E. Forget, P. V. Hofmeyer, L. S. Kenefic, C. Larouche, G. Lessard, J-M. Lussier, F. Pinto, J-C. Ruel, and A. Weiskittel. 2012. *Silvicultural Guide for Northern White-Cedar (Eastern White Cedar)* (General Technical Report NRS-98). Newtown Square, PA: U.S. Department of Agriculture, Forest Service, Northern Research Station.

Bourdo, E. A., Jr. 1983. "The Forest the Settlers Saw." In *The Great Lakes Forest: An Environmental and Social History*, edited by S. L. Flader, 3–16. Minneapolis: University of Minnesota Press.

Brandenburg, J. 2003. *Looking for the Summer*. Chanhassen, MN: NorthWood Press.

Burakowski, E. A., C. P. Wake, B. Braswell, and D. P. Brown. 2008. "Trends in Wintertime Climate in the Northeastern United States, 1965–2005." *Journal of Geophysical Research* 113: D20114.

Burt, D. M., G. J. Roloff, and D. R. Etter. 2017. "Climate Factors Related to Localized Changes in Snowshoe Hare (*Lepus americanus*) Occupancy." *Canadian Journal of Zoology* 95, no. 1: 15–22.

Butler, B. J., J. H. Hewes, B. J. Dickinson, K. Andrejczyk, S. M. Butler, and M. Markowski-Lindsay. 2016. "Family Forest Ownerships of the United States, 2013: Findings from the USDA Forest Service's National Woodland Owner Survey." *Journal of Forestry* 114, no. 6: 638–647.

Chimner, R. A., D. J. Cooper, F. C. Wurster, and L. Rochefort. 2017. "An Overview of Peatland Restoration in North America: Where Are We after 25 Years?" *Restoration Ecology* 25, no. 2: 283–292.

Chimner, R. A., and J. B. Hart. 1996. "Hydrology and Microtopography Effects on Northern White-Cedar Regeneration in Michigan's Upper Peninsula." *Canadian Journal of Forest Research* 26: 389–393.

Clements, F. E. 1916. *Plant Succession: An Analysis of the Development of Vegetation*. Washington, DC: Carnegie Institution of Washington.

Cohen, J. G., M. A. Kost, B. S. Slaughter, and D. A. Albert. 2015. *A Field Guide to the Natural Communities of Michigan*. East Lansing: Michigan State University Press.

Connecticut Department of Energy and Environmental Protection. 2015. "Endangered, Threatened, and Special Concern Plants." https://portal.ct.gov/DEEP/Endangered-Species/Endangered-Species-Listings/Endangered-Threatened—Special-Concern-Plants.

Cornett, M. W., L. E. Frelich, K. J. Puettmann, and P. B. Reich. 2000. "Conservation Implications of Browsing by *Odocoileus virginianus* in Remnant Upland *Thuja occidentalis* Forests." *Biological Conservation* 93: 359–369.

Cornett, M. W., K. J. Puettmann, L. E. Frelich, and P. B. Reich. 2001. "Comparing the Importance of Seedbed and Canopy Type in the Restoration of Upland *Thuja occidentalis* Forests of Northeastern Minnesota." *Restoration Ecology* 9: 386–396.

Cornett, M. W., P. B. Reich, and K. J. Puettmann. 1997. "Canopy Feedbacks and Microtopography Regulate Conifer Seedling Distribution in Two Minnesota Conifer-Deciduous Forests." *Ecoscience* 4, no. 3: 353–364.

Culin, R. S. 1907. *Games of the North American Indians: Twenty-Fourth Annual Report of the Bureau of American Ethnology*. Washington, DC: Smithsonian Institution.

Curtis, J. D. 1946. "Preliminary Observations on Northern White Cedar in Maine." *Ecology* 27, no. 1: 23–36.

Curtis, J. T. 1959. *The Vegetation of Wisconsin: An Ordination of Plant Communities*. Madison: University of Wisconsin Press.

Dahlberg, B. L., and R. C. Guettinger. 1956. *The White-Tailed Deer in Wisconsin* (Technical Bulletin No. 14). Madison: Wisconsin Conservation Department.

Danielsen, K. C. 2002. *The Cultural Importance, Ecology, and Status of Giizhik (Northern White Cedar) in the Ceded Territories* (Administrative Report 02-06, April 2002). Odanah, WI: Great Lakes Indian Fish & Wildlife Commission, Biological Services Division.

Danneyrolles, V., S. Dupuis, D. Arseneault, R. Terrail, M. Leroyer, A. de Römer, G. André, G. Fortin, Y. Boucher, and J-C. Ruel. 2017. "Eastern White Cedar Long-Term Dynamics in Eastern Canada: Implications for Restoration in the Context of Ecosystem-Based Management." *Forest Ecology and Management* 400: 502–510.

Davis, M. B. 1990. "Climate Change and the Survival of Forest Species." In *The Earth in Transition: Patterns and Processes of Biotic Impoverishment*, edited by G. M. Woodwell, 99–110. Cambridge: Cambridge University Press.

———, ed. 1996. *Eastern Old-Growth Forests: Prospects for Rediscovery and Recovery*. Washington, DC: Island Press.

Davis, R. B., and G. L. Jacobson Jr. 1985. "Late Glacial and Early Holocene Landscapes in Northern New England and Adjacent Areas of Canada." *Quaternary Research* 23: 341–368.

de Blois, S., and A. Bouchard. 1995. "Dynamics of *Thuja occidentalis* in an Agricultural Landscape of Southern Quebec." *Journal of Vegetation Science* 6: 531–542.

deCalesta, D. 2017. "Achieving and Maintaining Sustainable White-Tailed Deer Density with Adaptive Management." *Human–Wildlife Interactions* 11, no. 1: 99–111.

Densmore, F. 1974. *How Indians Use Wild Plants for Food, Medicine and Crafts*. New York: Dover Publications.

Doepker, R. V., and J. J. Ozoga. 1991. "Wildlife Values of Northern White-Cedar." In *1990 Workshop Proceedings for the Northern White-Cedar in Michigan* (Res. Rep. 512), edited by

D. O. Lantagne, 13–30. East Lansing: Michigan State University, Michigan Agricultural Experiment Station.

Durzan, D. J. 2009. "Arginine, Scurvy and Cartier's 'Tree of Life.'" *Journal of Ethnobiology and Ethnomedicine* 5.

Dyke, A. S., and V. K. Prest. 1987. "Late Wisconsinan and Holocene History of the Laurentide Ice Sheet." *Geographie Physique et Quaternaire* 41, no. 2: 237–263.

Eastman, J. 1995. *The Book of Swamp and Bog: Trees, Shrubs, and Wildflowers of Eastern Freshwater Wetlands.* Mechanicsburg, PA: Stackpole Books.

Epstein, E. E. 2017. "Chapter 7: Natural Communities, Aquatic Features, and Selected Habitats of Wisconsin." In *The Ecological Landscapes of Wisconsin: An Assessment of Ecological Resources and a Guide to Planning Sustainable Management* (PUB-SS-1131H 2017). Madison: Wisconsin Department of Natural Resources.

Epstein, E. E., E. J. Judziewicz, and E. A. Spencer. 2002. *Wisconsin Natural Community Abstracts.* Madison: Wisconsin Department of Natural Resources, Bureau of Endangered Resources.

Erickson, A. W. 1955. "An Ecological Study of the Bobcat in Michigan." MS thesis, Michigan State University.

Faber-Langendoen, D. 2001. "Plant Communities of the Midwest: Classification in an Ecological Context." Arlington, VA: Association for Biodiversity Information. https://www.natureserve.org/sites/default/files/plant-communities-midwest.pdf.

Flader, S. L., ed. 1983. *The Great Lakes Forest: An Environmental and Social History.* Minneapolis: University of Minnesota Press.

Forester, J. D., D. P. Anderson, and M. G. Turner. 2008. "Landscape and Local Factors Affecting Northern White Cedar (*Thuja occidentalis*) Recruitment in the Chequamegon-Nicolet National Forest, Wisconsin (U.S.A.)." *American Midland Naturalist* 160: 438–453.

Fowells, H. A., comp. 1965. *Silvics of Forest Trees of the United States* (Agricultural Handbook 271). Washington, DC: U.S. Department of Agriculture.

Fraver, S., L. S. Kenefic, A. Cutko, and A. S. White. 2020. "Natural Disturbance and Stand Structure of Old-Growth Northern White-Cedar Forests, Northern Maine, USA." *Forest Ecology and Management* 456.

Gawler, S., and A. Cutko. 2010. *Natural Landscapes of Maine: A Guide to Natural Communities and Ecosystems.* Augusta: Maine Department of Conservation, Maine Natural Areas Program.

Gordon, J. 1993. *Construction and Reconstruction of a Mi'kmaq Sixteenth-Century Cedar-Bark Bag.* Halifax: Nova Scotia Department of Education, Nova Scotia Museum.

Greller, A. M. 2000. "Vegetation in the Floristic Regions of North and Central America." In *Imperfect Balance: Landscape Transformations in the Pre-Columbian Americas*, edited by D. L. Lentz, 39–87. New York: Columbia University Press.

Grotte, K. 2007. "Old-Growth Northern White-Cedar (*Thuja occidentalis* L.) Stands in the Mid-Boreal Lowlands of Manitoba." Honours thesis, Department of Biology, University of Winnipeg.

Habeck, J. R., and J. T. Curtis. 1959. "Forest Cover and Deer Population Densities in Early Northern Wisconsin." *Wisconsin Academy of Sciences, Arts, and Letters* 48: 49–56.

Handler, S., M. J. Duveneck, L. Iverson, E. Peters, R. M. Scheller, K. R. Wythers, L. Brandt, P. Butler, M. Janowiak, P. D. Shannon et al. 2014a. *Michigan Forest Ecosystem Vulnerability Assessment and Synthesis: A Report from the Northwoods Climate Change Response Framework Project.* (General Technical Report NRS-129). Newtown Square, PA: U.S. Department of Agriculture, Forest Service, Northern Research Station.

———. 2014b. *Minnesota Forest Ecosystem Vulnerability Assessment and Synthesis: A Report from the Northwoods Climate Change Response Framework Project.* (Gen. Tech. Rep. NRS-133). Newtown Square, PA: U.S. Department of Agriculture, Forest Service, Northern Research Station.

Hannah, P. R. 2004. "Stand Structures and Height Growth Patterns in Northern White Cedar Stands on Wet Sites in Vermont." *Northern Journal of Applied Forestry* 21, no. 4: 173–179.

Hayhoe, K., C. P. Wake, T. G. Huntington, L. Luo, M. D. Schwartz, J. Sheffield, E. Wood, B. Anderson, J. Bradbury, A. DeGaetano, T. J. Troy, and D. Wolf. 2007. "Past and Future Changes in Climate and Hydrological Indicators in US Northeast." *Climate Dynamics* 28: 381–407.

Heinrichs, D. K. 2009. "Ecology of Northern White-Cedar (*Thuja occidentalis* L.) Stands at Their Northwestern Limit of Distribution in Manitoba, Canada." MS thesis, University of Manitoba.

Heinselman, M. 1996. *The Boundary Waters Wilderness Ecosystem.* Minneapolis: University of Minnesota Press.

Heitzman, E., K. S. Pregitzer, and R. O. Miller. 1997. "Origin and Early Development of Northern White-Cedar Stands in Northern Michigan." *Canadian Journal of Forest Research* 27: 1953–1961.

Heitzman, E., K. S. Pregitzer, R. O. Miller, M. Lanasa, and M. Zuidema. 1999. "Establishment and Development of Northern White-Cedar Following Strip Clearcutting." *Forest Ecology and Management* 123: 97–104.

Hennon, P. E., D. V. D'Amore, P. G. Schaberg, D. T. Wittwer, and C. S. Shanley. 2012. "Shifting Climate, Altered Niche, and a Dynamic Conservation Strategy for Yellow-Cedar in the North Pacific Coastal Rainforest." *BioScience* 62: 147–158.

Herfindal, I., J-P. Tremblay, A. J. Hester, U. S. Lande, and H. K. Wam. 2015. "Associational Relationships at Multiple Spatial Scales Affect Forest Damage by Moose." *Forest Ecology and Management* 348: 97–107.

Hofmeyer, P. V., L. S. Kenefic, and R. S. Seymour. 2007. "Northern White-Cedar (*Thuja occidentalis* L): An Annotated Bibliography." University of Maine, Cooperative Forestry Research Unit.

———. 2009. "Northern White-Cedar Ecology and Silviculture in the Northeastern United States and Southeastern Canada: A Synthesis of Knowledge." *Northern Journal of Applied Forestry* 26: 21–27.

———. 2010. "Historical Stem Development of Northern White-Cedar (*Thuja occidentalis* L.) in Maine." *Northern Journal of Applied Forestry* 27: 92–96.

Hoover, W. 1991. "The Importance of Cedar in Michigan's Forest History." In *1990 Workshop Proceedings for the Northern White-Cedar in Michigan* (Res. Rep. 512), edited by D. O. Lantagne, 3–6. East Lansing: Michigan State University, Michigan Agricultural Experiment Station.

Horwitz, E. L. 1980. *On the Land: American Agriculture from Past to Present*. New York: Atheneum.

Hunter, M. L., Jr. 1989. "What Constitutes an Old-Growth Stand?" *Journal of Forestry* 87: 33–35.

Indiana Department of Natural Resources. 2020. Indiana Natural Heritage Data Center. "Endangered Plant and Species." https://www.in.gov/dnr/nature-preserves/heritage-data-center/endangered-plant-and-animal-species/.

Iverson, L., A. Prasad, and S. Matthews. 2008. "Modeling Potential Climate Change Impacts on the Trees of the Northeastern United States." *Mitigation and Adaptation Strategies for Global Change* 13: 517–540.

Janowiak, M. K., A. W. D'Amato, C. W. Swanston, L. Iverson, F. R. Thompson, W. D. Dijak, S. Matthews, M. P. Peters, A. Prasad, J. S. Fraser et al. 2018. *New England and Northern New York Forest Ecosystem Vulnerability Assessment and Synthesis: A Report from the New England Climate Change Response Framework Project*. (Gen. Tech. Rep. NRS-173). Newtown Square, PA: U.S. Department of Agriculture, Forest Service, Northern Research Station.

Janowiak, M. K., L. R. Iverson, D. J. Mladenoff, E. Peters, K. R. Wythers, W. Xi, L. A. Brandt, P. R. Butler, S. D. Handler, P. D. Shannon et al. 2014. *Forest Ecosystem Vulnerability Assessment and Synthesis for Northern Wisconsin and Western Upper Michigan: A Report from the Northwoods Climate Change Response Framework Project* (Gen. Tech. Rep. NRS-136). Newtown Square, PA: U.S. Department of Agriculture, Forest Service, Northern Research Station.

Janssen, C. R. 1968. "Myrtle Lake: A Late- and Post-Glacial Pollen Diagram from Northern Minnesota." *Canadian Journal of Botany* 46: 1397–1408.

Johnson, R. S. 1986. *Forests of Nova Scotia: A History*. Halifax: Nova Scotia Department of Lands and Forests/Four East Publications.

Johnston, W. F. 1972. *Balsam Fir Dominant Species under Rethinned Northern White-Cedar* (Research Note NC-133). U.S. Department of Agriculture, Forest Service, North Central Experiment Station.

———. 1977. *Manager's Handbook for Northern White-Cedar in the North Central States* (General Technical Report NC-35). St. Paul, MN: U.S. Department of Agriculture, North Central Forest Experimental Station.

———. 1980. "Northern White-Cedar." In *Forest Cover Types of the United States and Canada*, edited by F. H. Eyre, 23–24. Washington, DC: Society of American Foresters.

———. 1990. "*Thuja occidentalis* L.—Northern White-Cedar." In *Silvics of North America*, vol. 1 (Agricultural Handbook 654), by R. M. Burns and B. H. Honkala, technical coordinators, 580–589. Washington, DC: U.S. Department of Agriculture, Forest Service.

Johnston, W. F., and R. G. Booker. 1983. "Northern White-Cedar." In *Silvicultural Systems for the Major Forest Types of the United States* (Agricultural Handbook 445), edited by R. M. Burns, 105–108. Washington, DC: U.S. Department of Agriculture, Forest Service.

Judd, R. W. 1989. *Aroostook: A Century of Logging in Northern Maine*. Orono: University of Maine Press.

Jules, H. A., Y. Bergeron, and A. Ali. 2018. "Are Marginal Balsam Fir and Eastern White Cedar Stands Relics from Once More Extensive Populations in North-Eastern North America?" *The Holocene* 28, no. 10: 1672–1679.

Kangas, L. C., R. Schwartz, M. R. Pennington, C. R. Webster, and R. A. Chimner. 2016. "Artificial Microtopography and Herbivory Protection Facilitates Wetland Tree (*Thuja occidentalis* L.) Survival and Growth in Created Wetlands." *New Forests* 47: 73–86.

Kell, J. 2009. "Soil-Site Influences on Northern White-Cedar (*Thuja occidentalis* L.) Stem Quality." MS thesis, University of Maine.

Kenefic, L., A. R. Kizha, S. Fraver, A. Roth, J. Wason, K. Kanoti. 2020. "Silviculture and Operations in Northern White-Cedar Lowlands." In *Cooperative Forestry Research Unit: 2019 Annual Report*, edited by S. M. Anderson and M. Fergusson, 13–21. Orono: Center for Research on Sustainable Forests, University of Maine.

Kincaid, J. A. 2017. "The Effects of Climate on Radial Growth of Disjunct Northern White Cedar (*Thuja occidentalis* L.) in Virginia." *Virginia Journal of Science* 68, no. 3–4.

Knapp, S. 2019. "Are Humans Really Blind to Plants?" *Plants, People, Planet*, no. 1: 164–168.

Kost, M. A. 2002. *Natural Community Abstract for Rich Conifer Swamp*. Lansing: Michigan Natural Features Inventory.

Kost, M. A., D. A. Albert, J. G. Cohen, B. S. Slaughter, R. K. Schillo, C. R. Weber, and K. A. Chapman. 2007. *Natural Communities of Michigan: Classification and Description*. (Report Number 2007-21). Lansing: Michigan State University, Michigan Natural Features Inventory.

LaCrosse Tribune. 2014. "Officials May Suspend Doe Hunt in State." *LaCrosse Tribune*, May 15.

Larouche, C., L. Kenefic, and J-C. Ruel. 2010. "Northern White-Cedar Regeneration Dynamics on the Penobscot Experimental Forest in Maine: 40 Year Results." *Northern Journal of Applied Forestry* 27: 5–12.

Larouche, C., and J-C. Ruel. 2015. "Development of Northern White-Cedar Regeneration Following Partial Cutting, with and without Deer Browsing." *Forests* 6: 344–359.

Larouche, C., J-C. Ruel, and J-M. Lussier. 2011. "Factors Affecting Northern White-Cedar (*Thuja occidentalis*) Seedling Establishment and Early Growth in Mixedwood Stands." *Canadian Journal of Forest Research* 27: 1953–1961.

Larrieu L., Y. Paillet, S. Winter, R. Bütler, D. Kraus, F. Krumm et al. 2018. "Tree Related Microhabitats in Temperate and Mediterranean European Forests: A Hierarchical Typology for Inventory Standardization." *Ecological Indicators* 84: 194–207.

Larson, D. W., J. Doubt, and U. Matthes-Sears. 1994. "Radially Sectored Hydraulic Pathways in the Xylem of *Thuja occidentalis* as Revealed by the Use of Dyes." *International Journal of Plant Sciences* 155, no. 5: 569–582.

Larson, D. W., and P. E. Kelly. 1991. "The Extent of Old-Growth *Thuja occidentalis* on Cliffs of the Niagara Escarpment." *Canadian Journal of Botany* 69: 1628–1636.

Larson, D. W., U. Matthes-Sears, and P. E. Kelly. 1993. "Cambial Dieback and Partial Shoot Mortality in Cliff-Face *Thuja occidentalis*: Evidence for Sectored Radial Architecture." *International Journal of Plant Sciences* 154, no. 4: 496–505.

Lemieux, M. J. 2010. *A Management Plan for Native Occurrences of Eastern White Cedar (Thuja occidentalis L.) in Nova Scotia*. Kentville, NS: Department of Natural Resources.

Leopold, A. 1949. *A Sand County Almanac*. New York: Oxford University Press.

Leopold, D. J., P. J. Smallidge, and J. D. Castello. 1996. "An Integrated Model of Forest Dynamics Following Disturbance." In *Forest: A Global Perspective*, edited by S. K. Majumdar, E. W. Miller, and F. J. Brenner, 63–78. Easton: Pennsylvania Academy of Science.

Linnaeus, C. 1735. *Systema naturæ, sive regna tria naturæ systematice proposita per classes, ordines, genera & species*. 1st ed. Leiden, Netherlands: T. Haak.

Lizotte, T. 1998. "Productivity, Survivorship, and Winter Feeding Ecology of an Experimentally Reintroduced Elk Herd in Northern Wisconsin." MS thesis, University of Wisconsin-Stevens Point.

Lovett, B. 2021. "Three Reasons Fungi Are Not Plants." *American Society for Microbiology*, 26 January. https://asm.org/Articles/2021/January/Three-Reasons-Fungi-Are-Not-Plants.

Lukkarinen, V. L. M. 2014. "Using Mosses to Assess Conditions in Northern White-Cedar Swamps." Master's thesis, Michigan Technological University. https://doi.org/10.37099/mtu.dc.etds/877.

Lussier, J-M., and P. Meek. 2014. "Managing Heterogeneous Stands Using a Multiple-Treatment Irregular Shelterwood Method." *Journal of Forestry* 112, no. 3: 287–295.

Maier, C. T. 2007. "Distribution and Hosts of *Callidiellum rufipenne* (Coleoptera: Cerambycidae), an Asian Cedar Borer Established in the Eastern United States." *Journal of Economic Entomology* 100, no. 4: 1291–1297.

Maine Department of Agriculture, Conservation and Forestry. 2015. "Rare, Threatened, and Endangered Plant Taxa." https://www.maine.gov/dacf/mnap/features/rare_plants/plantlist.htm.

Marrone, T. 2009. "Sugar from Trees." *Minnesota Conservation Volunteer* 72, no. 423: 54–65.

Maryland Department of Natural Resources, Natural Heritage Program. 2021. "List of Rare, Threatened, and Endangered Plants of Maryland." https://dnr.maryland.gov/wildlife/Documents/rte_Plant_List.pdf.

Massachusetts Division of Fisheries and Wildlife. 2020. "Massachusetts Endangered Species." https://www.mass.gov/doc/printable-list-of-endangered-threatened-and-special-concern-species/download.

Mattfeld, G. F. 1984. "Northeastern Hardwood and Spruce/Fir Forests." In *White-Tailed Deer: Ecology and Management*, edited by L. K. Halls, 305–330. Harrisburg, PA: Stackpole Books.

McCabe, R. E., and T. R. McCabe. 1984. "Of Slings and Arrows: An Historical Retrospective." In *White-Tailed Deer: Ecology and Management*, edited by L. K. Halls, 19–72. Harrisburg, PA: Stackpole Books.

McCaffery, K. 1986. "On Deer Carrying Capacity in Northern Wisconsin." In *Proceedings of the 22nd Northeast Deer Technical Committee*, 54–69. Waterbury: Vermont Fish and Wildlife Department.

Meiggs, R. 1982. *Trees and Timber in the Ancient Mediterranean World*. Oxford: Clarendon Press.

Michigan State University. n.d. "Michigan's Rare Plants." https://mnfi.anr.msu.edu/species/plants.

Miller, R. O. 1990. "Ecology and Management of Northern White-Cedar." Presented at the "Regenerating Conifer Cover in Deer Yards" Workshop. Ontario, Canada.

Miller, R. O., D. Elsing, M. Lanasa, and M. Zuidema. 1991. "Northern White-Cedar: Stand Assessment and Management Options." In *1990 Workshop Proceedings for the Northern White-Cedar in Michigan* (Res. Rep. 512), edited by D. O. Lantagne, 47–56. East Lansing: Michigan State University, Michigan Agricultural Experiment Station.

Milner, G. R., and G. Chaplin. 2010. "Eastern North American Population at ca. A.D. 1500." *American Antiquity* 75, no. 4: 707–726.

Minnesota Department of Natural Resources. 1996. *Inventory of Biological Features in O. L. Kipp State Park* (Biological Report Number 55). Prepared for the Division of Parks and Recreation by the Minnesota County Biological Survey, August 1996. St. Paul: Minnesota Department of Natural Resources.

———. 2003. *Field Guide to the Native Plant Communities of Minnesota: The Laurentian Mixed Forest Province*. Ecological Land Classification Program. Minnesota County Biological Survey, and Natural Heritage and Nongame Research Program. St. Paul: Minnesota Department of Natural Resources.

———. 2005. *Great River Bluffs State Park Management Plan*. St. Paul: Minnesota Department of Natural Resources.

———. 2019. *Forest Health Annual Report 2018*. St. Paul: Minnesota Department of Natural Resources.

———. n.d. "Minnesota's Endangered, Threatened, and Special Concern Species." https://www.dnr.state.mn.us/ets/index.html.

Minnesota Historical Society. "Maple Sugaring and the Ojibwe." https://www.mnopedia.org/thing/maple-sugaring-and-ojibwe.

Mittleman, E. B. 1923. "The Gyppo System." *Journal of Political Economy* 31, no. 6: 840–851.

Moen, A. N. 1973. *Wildlife Ecology: An Analytical Approach.* San Francisco: W. H. Freeman and Company.

Moore, M. I. 1978. "Eastern White Pine and Eastern White Cedar." *Forestry Chronicle* (August): 222–223.

Moran, R. J. 1973. *The Rocky Mountain Elk in Michigan.* (Res. Dev. Rep. 267). Lansing: Michigan Department of Natural Resources.

Mosseler, A., J. A. Lynds, and J. E. Major. 2003. "Old-Growth Forests of the Acadian Forest Region." *Environmental Reviews* 11, no. S1: S47–S77.

Müller-Schwarze, D. 2011. *The Beaver: Its Life and Impact.* 2nd ed. Ithaca, NY: Cornell University Press.

Natural Resources Canada. 2015. "Arborvitae leafminer." Ottawa: Natural Resources Canada, Canadian Forest Service. https://tidcf.nrcan.gc.ca/en/insects/factsheet/12117.

Nelson, T. C. 1951. *A Reproduction Study of Northern White Cedar Including Results of Investigations under Federal Aid in Wildlife Restoration Project Michigan 49-R.* Lansing: Michigan Department of Conservation.

New Jersey Division of Parks and Forestry. 2016. "List of Endangered Plant Species and Plant Species of Special Concern." https://www.state.nj.us/dep/parksandforests/natural/heritage/njplantlist.pdf.

New York Natural Heritage Program. 2021. Online Conservation Guide for Northern White Cedar Swamp. https://guides.nynhp.org/northern-white-cedar-swamp/.

Nolte, D. L., K. K. Wagner, and A. Trent. 2003. "Timber Damage by Black Bears." U.S. Department of Agriculture, National Wildlife Research Center—Staff Publications 257. https://digitalcommons.unl.edu/icwdm_usdanwrc/257.

Nova Scotia Department of Natural Resources. 2010. "A Management Plan for Native Occurrences of Eastern White Cedar (*Thuja occidentalis* L.) in Nova Scotia." Kentville, Nova Scotia, Canada: Nova Scotia Department of Natural Resources, Wildlife Division. https://novascotia.ca/natr/wildlife/biodiversity/pdf/Management_Plan_EWC_NS_July_2010_MJL.pdf.

Nutting, A. D. 1949. *Twenty-Eighth Biennial Report of the Forest Commissioner of the State of Maine.* Augusta: State of Maine, 88–89.

Odum, E. P. 1969. "The Strategy of Ecosystem Development." *Science* 164: 262–270.

Office of Kentucky Natural Preserves, Kentucky Energy and Environment Cabinet. 2019. "Endangered, Threatened, and Special Concern Plants, Animals, and Natural Communities of Kentucky." https://eec.ky.gov/Nature-Preserves/biodiversity/Documents/Rare_species_of_Kentucky.pdf.

Ott, C. A., and R. A. Chimner. 2016. "Long-Term Peat Accumulation in Temperate Forested Peatlands (*Thuja occidentalis* Swamps) in the Great Lakes Region of North America." *Mires and Peat* 18: 1–9.

Palik, B. J., B. K. Haworth, A. J. David, and R. K. Kolka. 2015. "Survival and Growth of Northern White-Cedar and Balsam Fir Seedlings in Riparian Management Zones in Northern
Minnesota, USA." *Forest Ecology and Management* 337: 20–27.

Patterson, J. E. H., S. J. Patterson, and J. R. Malcolm. 2007. "Cavity Nest Materials of Northern
Flying Squirrels, *Glaucomys sabrinus*, and North American Red Squirrels, *Tamiasciurus
hudsonicus*, in a Secondary Hardwood Forest of Southern Ontario." *Canadian Field-
Naturalist* 121: 303–307.

Pinkerton, K. 1947. *Bright with Silver*. New York: William Sloane Associates.

Prasad A., J. Pedlar, M. Peters, D. McKenney, L. Iverson, S. Matthews, and B. Adams. 2020a.
"Combining U.S. and Canadian Forest Inventories to Assess Habitat Suitability and
Migration Potential of 25 Tree Species under Climate Change." *Diversity and Distribu-
tions* 26: 1142–1159.

———. 2020b. "Data from: Combining U.S. and Canadian Forest Inventories to Assess
Habitat Suitability and Migration Potential of 25 Tree Species under Climate Change."
Dryad. https://doi.org/10.5061/dryad.qz612jmbn.

Pregitzer, K. S. 1991. "The Ecology of Northern White-Cedar." In *1990 Workshop Proceedings
for the Northern White-Cedar in Michigan* (Res. Rep. 512), edited by D. O. Lantagne,
7–12. East Lansing: Michigan State University, Michigan Agricultural Experiment
Station.

Radeloff, V. C., R. B. Hammer, and S. I. Stewart. 2005. "Rural and Suburban Sprawl in the
U.S. Midwest from 1940 to 2000 and Its Relation to Forest Fragmentation." *Conservation
Biology* 19, no. 3: 793–805.

Rayfield, B., V. Paul, F. Tremblay, M. Fortin, C. Hély, and Y. Bergeron. 2021. "Influence of
Habitat Availability and Fire Disturbance on a Northern Range Boundary." *Journal of
Biogeography* 48 2: 394–404.

Rhemtulla, J. M., D. J. Mladenoff, and M. K. Clayton. 2009. "Legacies of Historical Land Use
on Regional Forest Composition and Structure in Wisconsin, USA (Mid-1800s–1930s–
2000s)." *Ecological Applications* 19: 1061–1078.

Rooney, T. P. 2001. "Deer Impacts on Forest Ecosystems: A North American Perspective."
Forestry 74: 201–208.

Rooney, T. P., S. L. Solheim, and D. M. Waller. 2002. "Factors Affecting the Regeneration of
Northern White-Cedar in Lowland Forests of the Upper Great Lakes Region, USA."
Forest Ecology and Management 163: 119–130.

Rooney, T. P., and D. M. Waller. 2003. "Direct and Indirect Effects of White-Tailed Deer in
Forest Ecosystems." *Forest Ecology and Management* 181: 165–176.

Ruel, J-C., J-M. Lussier, S. Morissette, and N. Rocodeau. 2014. "Growth Response of Northern
White-Cedar (*Thuja occidentalis*) to Natural Disturbances and Partial Cuts in Mixedwood Stands in Quebec, Canada." *Forests* 5: 1194–1211.

Rusterholz, K. A. 1996. "Identification and Protection of Old Growth on State-Owned Land in Minnesota." In *Eastern Old-Growth Forests*, edited by M. B. Davis, 233–244. Washington, DC: Island Press.

Safford, L. O., J. C. Bjorkbom, and J. C. Zasada. 1990. "*Betula papyrifera* Marsh, Paper Birch." In *Silvics of North America*, vol. 2, *Hardwoods*, by R. M. Burns and B. H. Honkala, technical coordinators, 158–171. Agriculture Handbook 654. Washington, DC: U.S. Department of Agriculture, Forest Service.

Sandberg, L. 1983. "The Response of Forest Industries to a Changing Environment." In *The Great Lakes Forest: An Environmental and Social History*, edited by S. L. Flader, 194–204. Minneapolis: University of Minnesota Press.

Sanders-DeMott, R., J. L. Campbell, P. M. Groffman, L. E. Rustad, and P. H. Templer. 2019. "Soil Warming and Winter Snowpacks: Implications for Northern Forest Ecosystem Functioning." In *Ecosystem Consequences of Soil Warming: Microbes, Vegetation, Fauna and Soil Biogeochemistry*, edited by J. E. Mohan, 245–278. Cambridge, MA: Academic Press.

Saucier, L., J-C. Ruel, and C. Larouche. 2018. "Variations in Northern White-Cedar (*Thuja occidentalis*) Regeneration Following Operational Selection Cutting in Mixedwood Stands of Western Quebec." *Canadian Journal of Forest Research* 48, no. 11: 1311–1319.

Schaffer, W. W. 1996. *Silvicultural Guidelines for the Eastern White-Cedar*. (Tech. Rep. TR-006). Peterborough: Ontario Ministry of Natural Resources, Southern Region Science and Technology Transfer Unit.

Schopmeyer, C. S. 1974. "*Thuja* L. (Arborvitae)." In *Seeds of Woody Plants in the United States* (Agric. Handbook No. 450), edited by C. S. Schopmeyer, 805–809. Washington, DC: U.S. Department of Agriculture, Forest Service.

Selva, S. B. 2003. "Using Calicioid Lichens and Fungi to Assess Ecological Continuity in the Acadian Forest Ecoregion of the Canadian Maritimes." *Forestry Chronicle* 79: 550–558.

Silver, G. T. 1957. "Studies on the Arborvitae Leaf Miners in New Brunswick (Lepidoptera: Yponomeutidae and Gelechiidae)." *Canadian Entomologist* 89, no. 4: 171–182.

Simard, M., Y. Bergeron, and L. Sirois. 2003. "Substrate and Litterfall Effects on Conifer Seedling Survivorship in Southern Boreal Stands of Canada." *Canadian Journal of Forest Research* 33: 672–681.

Skatter, S., and B. Kucera. 1998. "The Cause of the Prevalent Directions of the Spiral Grain Patterns in Conifers." *Trees* 12: 265–273.

Smallidge, P. J., and B. J. Chedzoy. 2019. "Slash Walls to Protect Forest Regeneration: Contracts, Costs and Preliminary Effectiveness." Presentation to the New England Society of American Foresters, Burlington, VT, 28 March 2019. Images and narration at http://CornellForestConnect.ning.com.

Smith, R. 2017. "Plant Species Richness and Diversity of Northern White-Cedar (*Thuja occidentalis*) Swamps in Northern New York: Effects and Interactions of Multiple Variables." MS thesis, State University of New York College of Environmental Science and Forestry.

Stanton, D. C. 1963. *A History of the White-Tailed Deer in Maine* (Bulletin No. 8). Augusta: Maine Game Division.

Stearns, F. W. 1997. "History of the Lake States Forests: Natural and Human Impacts." In *Lake States Regional Forest Resources Assessment: Technical Papers* (Gen. Tech. Rep. NC-189), edited by J. M. Vasievich and H. H. Webster. St. Paul, MN: U.S. Department of Agriculture, North Central Forest Experimental Station.

Storm, G. L., and W. L. Palmer. 1995. "White-Tailed Deer in the Northeast." In *Our Living Resources: A Report to the Nation on the Distribution, Abundance, and Health of U.S. Plants, Animals, and Ecosystems*, edited by E. T. LaRoe, G. S. Farris, C. E. Puckett, P. D. Doran, and M. J. Mac, 112–115. Washington, DC: U.S. Department of the Interior, National Biological Service.

Swift, E. 1946. *A History of Wisconsin Deer* (Publication 323). Madison: Wisconsin Conservation Department.

Tester, J. R. 1995. *Minnesota's Natural Heritage: An Ecological Perspective*. Minneapolis: University of Minnesota Press.

Thornton, P. L. 1957. "Problems of Managing Upper Michigan's Coniferous Swamps." *Journal of Forestry* 55: 192–197.

USDA Forest Service. 2012, 2018, and 2019. Forest Inventory and Analysis Program. https://apps.fs.usda.gov/fia/datamart/datamart_excel.html.

USDA Natural Resources Conservation Service. 2019 and 2021. "The PLANTS Database." http://plants.usda.gov.

Van Deelen, T. 1999. "Deer-Cedar Interactions during a Period of Mild Winters: Implications for Conservation of Conifer Swamp Deeryards in the Great Lakes Region." *Natural Areas Journal* 19: 263–274.

Verme, L. J., and W. F. Johnston. 1986. "Regeneration of Northern White Cedar Deeryards in Upper Michigan." *Journal of Wildlife Management* 50: 307–313.

Villemaire-Côté, O., J-C. Ruel, and L. Sirois. 2017. "Development of Northern White-Cedar (*Thuja occidentalis* L.) Plantations within and outside Deer Yards." *Forests* 8, no. 9: 326.

Waller, D. M. 2008. "White-Tailed Deer Impacts in North America and the Challenge of Managing a Hyperabundant Herbivore." In *Lessons from the Islands: Introduced Species and What They Tell Us about How Ecosystems Work*, edited by A. J. Gaston, T. E. Golumbia, J-L. Martin, and S. T. Sharpe, 135–147. Ottawa: Canadian Wildlife Service, Environment Canada.

Wandersee, J. H., and E. E. Schussler. 2001. "Toward a Theory of Plant Blindness." *Plant Science Bulletin* 47, no. 1: 2–9.

WCCO. 2015. "Finding Minnesota: North Shore's 'Witch Tree.'" CBS Minnesota, 25 October 2015. https://minnesota.cbslocal.com/2015/10/25/finding-minnesota-north-shores-witch-tree/.

Wesely, N., S. Fraver, L. S. Kenefic, A. R. Weiskittel, J-C. Ruel, M. E. Thompson, and A. S. White. 2018. "Structural Attributes of Old-Growth and Partially Harvested Northern White-Cedar Stands in Northeastern North America." *Forests* 9, no. 7: 376.

West Virginia Division of Natural Resources. 2020. "Rare Plants Tracked by the West Virginia Natural Heritage Program." http://www.wvdnr.gov/Wildlife/PDFFiles/RTE_Plants.

Williamson, D. 1976. *Give 'er Snoose: A Study of Kin and Work among Gyppo Loggers of the Pacific Northwest*. Washington, DC: Catholic University of America Press.

Wilson, B. T., A. J. Lister, R. I. Riemann, and D. M. Griffith. 2013. "Live Tree Species Basal Area of the Contiguous United States (2000–2009)." Newtown Square, PA: USDA Forest Service, Rocky Mountain Research Station. https://doi.org/10.2737/RDS-2013-0013.

Wisconsin Department of Natural Resources. 1998. *Wisconsin's Deer Management Program: The Issues Involved in Decision Making*. 2nd ed. Madison: Wisconsin Department of Natural Resources.

———. 2019. *Silviculture Handbook* (Publication No. HB24315). Madison: Wisconsin Department of Natural Resources.

———. n.d. "Population Goals." https://dnr.wi.gov/topic/WildlifeHabitat/documents/DTR/populationgoals.

———. n.d. "Wisconsin's Rare Plants." https://dnr.wi.gov/topic/endangeredresources/plants.asp.

Wood, R. 1935. *A History of Lumbering in Maine (1820–1861)*. Orono: University of Maine Press.

Yu, Z. 1997. "Late Quaternary Paleoecology of *Thuja* and *Juniperus* (Cupressaceae) at Crawford Lake, Ontario, Canada: Pollen, Stomata, and Macrofossils." *Review of Paleobotany and Palynology* 96: 241–254.

Zenner, E. K., and J. C. Almendinger. 2012. "Identifying Restoration Opportunities for Northern White Cedar by Contrasting Historical and Modern Inventories in an Ecological Classification System Context." *Ecological Restoration* 30, no. 3: 169–179.

LIST OF CONTRIBUTORS

Jeanette Allogio, ecologist and data manager, Center for Research on Sustainable Forests, University of Maine, Orono, Maine

Emmanuelle Boulfroy, project leader and research forester, applied forest ecology and agroforestry, Centre d'enseignement et de recherche en foresterie de Sainte-Foy inc., Quebec

Rod A. Chimner, professor of wetland ecology, School of Forest Resources and Environmental Science, Michigan Technological University, Houghton, Michigan

Christel C. Kern, research forester, U.S. Forest Service, Northern Research Station, Rhinelander, Wisconsin

Catherine Larouche, director of Scientific Support Division, Ministère des Forêts, de la Faune et des Parcs, Quebec

Guy Lessard, director and research forester, sustainable forest management and silviculture, Centre d'enseignement et de recherche en foresterie de Sainte-Foy inc., Quebec

Keith R. McCaffery, deer research biologist (retired), Wisconsin Department of Natural Resources, Rhinelander, Wisconsin

Charles Tardif, vice president, Corporate Development and Procurement, Maibec, Levis, Quebec

Justin Waskiewicz, assistant professor of forestry, Paul Smith's College, Paul Smiths, New York

Jay Wason, assistant professor of forest ecosystem physiology, School of Forest Resources, University of Maine, Orono, Maine

Christopher W. Woodall, research forester, U.S. Forest Service, Northern Research Station, Durham, New Hampshire

ABOUT THE AUTHORS

GERALD L. STORM, a native of Wisconsin, was raised on a dairy farm in Corning Township, Lincoln County. He spent five years with the Illinois Natural History Survey as a field ecologist. He was a wildlife biologist with the U.S. Department of Interior (Fish and Wildlife Service and National Biological Service) and served as an associate professor of wildlife management with Pennsylvania State University for twenty-five years, retiring in 1997. He was a member of The Wildlife Society for more than fifty years.

LAURA S. KENEFIC spent her early years in upstate New York before moving to Maine as a graduate student. She has been a research forester with the U.S. Forest Service, Northern Research Station for more than twenty years and is a faculty associate at the University of Maine. She studies sustainable management of northern forests and coleads a northern white-cedar research program informally called the Cedar Club. She has authored more than one hundred scientific and technical publications and has been recognized for her contributions to the education of natural resource managers and support of women in forestry.

INDEX